Rectifying the State of Israel

A Political Platform based on Kabbalah

THE TEACHINGS OF KABBALAH SERIES

By Rabbi Yitzchak Ginsburgh
(in English)

The Hebrew Letters
Channels of Creative Consciousness

The Mystery of Marriage
How to Find True Love and Happiness in Marriage

Awakening the Spark Within
Five Dynamics of Leadership that can Change the World

Transforming Darkness into Light
Kabbalah and Psychology

Rectifying the State of Israel
A Political Platform based on Kabbalah

Coming Soon:

Living in Divine Space
Kabbalah and Meditation

The Spirit of Life
Kabbalah and Medicine

Rectifying the State of Israel

A Political Platform based on Kabbalah

Rabbi Yitzchak Ginsburgh

Linda Pinsky Publications

a division of Gal Einai
Jerusalem

Printed in Israel
Second Edition

Copyright © 5763 (2003) by Gal Einai Institute

The Menorah on the cover was photographed courtesy of Rabbi Yisrael
Levanoni and Brit Shalom Publications.

For information address:

USA: Gal Einai Institute, Inc.
        PO Box 41
        Cedarhurst, NY 11516,
        tel/fax (toll-free): (888) 453-0571

Israel: Gal Einai
        PO Box 1015
        Kefar Chabad 72915
        tel.: (02) 996-1123; fax: (02) 996-2111

E-mail: inner@inner.org

Web: www.inner.org

Gal Einai publishes and produces books, pamphlets, audiocassettes and
videocassettes by Rabbi Yitzchak Ginsburgh. To receive a catalog of our
products in English and/or Hebrew, please contact us at any of the above
addresses, email orders@inner.org, or visit www.inner-store.org.

THIS BOOK IS PUBLISHED
IN LOVING MEMORY OF

RAPHAEL AND RACHEL
HORN

MAY THEIR SOULS BI BOUND UP IN THE
BOND OF ETERNAL LIFE

ת. נ. צ. ב. ה.

Table of Contents

Preface

The profound and ancient teachings of Jewish mysticism—Kabbalah—speak of the urgent need to rectify the world, to pick up the pieces of our shattered dreams and mend the tattered fabric of our lives, both as individuals and as active contributors to humanity's destiny. But beyond pointing out the need to make changes, Kabbalah teaches us how to make these changes in ways that will be comprehensive and enduring, and that will proceed organically out of the present reality.

Kabbalah addresses the spiritual core of the physical reality of the world around us. It radiates Divine light and goodness, awakening the point of goodness innate in every aspect of created reality. It elevates reality to a level of consciousness sensitive enough to receive—to become a "vessel" for—Divine directives, the Torah's statutes, given for the ultimate benefit of humanity.[1]

Today, the need to rectify reality is perhaps felt most acutely in Israel, where the dream of Jewish security and cultural revival seems to be threatened as never before. The state is in desperate need of a breath of new life, a new vision of its purpose that can rekindle the hearts and imaginations of Jews and non-Jews around the world.

In this book, Rabbi Yitzchak Ginsburgh sets forth a conceptual and practical program for healing the ills of the present state of reality in the State of Israel. These proposals are at once profound and practical, born of intimate acquaintance with the pulse of the people as well as the failings of Israeli politics, and permeated by Hassidic optimism and love for the Jewish people as well as for all humanity.

❧   ❧   ❧

The greatest inspiration in conceiving the program presented here has been the teachings of the Lubavitcher Rebbe, Rabbi Menachem Mendel Schneersohn. For over four decades, the Rebbe (whom we will quote repeatedly and therefore refer to simply as "the Rebbe") unceasingly and passionately insisted that the only way to overcome the present crisis facing the Jewish people in the Land of Israel (and affecting the Jewish people, and all people, worldwide) is to unabashedly stand up before the world and proclaim that the entire Land of Israel belongs to the entire Jewish people by Divine right, as stated in the Torah.

The Rebbe also insisted that important as Torah study, prayer, and observing the commandments are—and despite the essential role they play in safeguarding the security of the Jewish people everywhere, especially in the Land of Israel— they alone cannot constitute our entire response to our enemies' designs. We must take action. Rabbis who know the Torah's directives for all situations must assume their responsibility to inform the public and the politicians of the these directives. This is not "mixing religion with politics"; activism itself is a commandment.[2] And so, the Rebbe stands out in our generation not only as a profound thinker, but also as a staunch realist.

❧   ❧   ❧

It goes without saying that however critical the author is of secular Zionism's past, present, and agenda for the future, he should in no way be misconstrued as advocating the pitting of Jews against Jews (God forbid). The very opposite is true. It is the love for *all* Jews—and the faith that all Jews possess a Divine spark that will, sooner or later, arouse them to return to God and the Torah—that has motivated him to conceptualize the ideas presented here. Without faith, love, and hope for all, how can one even dream of *Rectifying the State of Israel*?

Moreover, who is ultimately to blame for the failures and evils of our own people? Though outwardly it may appear otherwise, it is the religious, believing Jew that must assume responsibility. The Torah commands us to love God,[3] which the sages interpret to mean that we should act in such ways that God becomes beloved by all.[4] If the conduct of a religious Jew does not attract his or her fellow Jews to live by the statutes of the Torah, then the religious Jew is to blame. Setting an admirable example for others is a sanctification of God's Name; not doing so is a desecration of God's Name.[5]

To begin the implementation of the program presented here, believing Jews must live their lives and relate to others according to the true spirit of the Torah, with humility toward all and manifest compassion for all.

❧   ❧   ❧

Rabbi Ginsburgh first presented the ideas on which this book is based in classes he gave in Yeshivat Od Yosef Chai, Shechem, in 1989. They were then published as an essay (*Machshavot Achadot Odot Matza Motzei Chen*, edited by Rabbi Yisrael Ariel) in the journal *Malchut Yisrael #8* (Gal Einai, 1991[6]). These ideas were then synopsized in an address to a convention held in Jerusalem in 1998. This address (transcribed by Mr. Itiel Giladi) was serialized in the periodical *Lechatchilah*, 2000. This article then appeared as an essay in a book entitled *Tipul Shoresh* (Gal Einai, 2001). This essay was translated into English by Ms. Judy Lee; new material was added to this translation, which appeared as the booklet, *The Rectification of the State of Israel: A Political Platform based on the Teachings of Kabbalah* (Gal Einai, 2002, 50 pp.). The present book is a much-enlarged expansion of that booklet.

In addition to the main flow of ideas in the text, *Rectifying the State of Israel* contains a wealth of more advanced material intended for seasoned students of Kabbalah and Hassidism. We have placed these expositions—some of which are complete essays in their own right—in endnotes at the end of the book. Even the beginner, however, will be enriched by perusing these notes.

෴   ෴   ෴

We have followed the following conventions in this book:

There are several Names for God used in the Bible and referred to here. Because of their holiness and spiritual power, it is forbidden to pronounce these Names other than in prayer or when reciting a complete Biblical verse. Therefore, we have deliberately altered the transliteration of these Names, in accordance with the time-honored practice of how observant Jews pronounce them in non-liturgical contexts.

The unique, four-letter Name of God is known generally as the Tetragrammaton and is referred to in Jewish writings (and in this book, as well) as "the Name *Havayah*." We are forbidden to pronounce this Name altogether, and indeed, its correct pronunciation is not known nowadays. In liturgical concepts, the Name *Adni* is pronounced in its place; in non-liturgical contexts, the word *Hashem* ("the Name") is substituted. Due to its special sanctity, it has been intentionally abbreviated (or hyphenated) when a verse is written-out in Hebrew. In English, we have spelled it with small capitals ("GOD") in order to distinguish it from all the other Names of God except for *Shakai*, which we translate as "the Almighty."

The term "Bible" (*Tanach*) comprises the Torah (the Five Books of Moses); the Prophets (consisting of eight books: Joshua, Judges, Samuel, Kings, Isaiah, Jeremiah, Ezekiel, and the Twelve Prophets); and the Writings (consisting of eleven books: Psalms, Proverbs, Job, Ruth, the Song of Songs, Ecclesiastes, Lamentations, Esther, Daniel, Ezra-Nehemiah, and Chronicles).

The term "Torah" must be understood according to the context: in its narrowest sense, it refers to the Five Books of Moses, but more generally, it can refer to the entirety of God's written and oral teachings to Israel and all of humanity.

The term "Kabbalah" is sometimes used in its specific sense, to refer to the classic texts of the ancient Jewish mystical tradition, and sometimes in its more general sense, to refer to the whole of the inner dimension of the Torah, including the teachings of Hassidism. Indeed, Hassidism is referred to in Hassidic texts as "the Kabbalah of the Ba'al Shem Tov,"[7] inasmuch as its revelation of the innermost core of faith and wisdom lies at the base of all the classic texts of Kabbalah (the *Zohar* and the writings of the holy Ari).

∋   ∋   ∋

We acknowledge here the invaluable editorial input of Rabbi and Mrs. Asher Crispe, Mr. Uri Kaploun, Ms. Uriela Obst, and Rabbi Moshe Wisnefsky, as well as the technical assistance of the entire Gal Einai staff.

We are deeply grateful to the Almighty for being able to offer the public this work. May the vision of the rectified State of Israel described in these pages be soon realized, and may we merit witnessing the full rectification of reality with the advent of the Messiah and the true and complete Redemption.

Jerusalem
18 Elul 5762

PART ONE

The Vision

ויאמר אלהים יהי אור

And God said, "Let there be Light"

—Genesis 1:3

CHAPTER ONE

It's Never Too Late

A MOMENTOUS MONTH

The State of Israel was established on the fifth day of the month of Iyar, 5708 (1948), when its founding fathers signed its Declaration of Independence. On this day, the Holy Land, promised by God to the Jewish people, was restored to Jewish sovereignty for the first time in nearly two thousand years. The fifth of Iyar is therefore known as Israel Independence Day (*Yom Ha'atzmaut*).

As momentous as this event was, the new country was devoid of its heart: ancient Jerusalem, the historic site of the Holy Temple and the focus of the Jewish people's life and prayers.

Then, on the twenty-eighth day of the same month, nineteen years later, ancient Jerusalem was liberated from the hands of the Arabs in the Six-Day War of 1967. On that day, the holiest city on earth was reunited under Jewish sovereignty—in the words of Psalms, "the city became joined together."[1] The twenty-eighth of Iyar is thus known as Jerusalem Day (*Yom Yerushalayim*).

Yet, despite these miraculous events, the modern State of Israel seems to be entangled in a deteriorating maze of crises. Terror and war threaten it on all sides. The custodians of the state daily surrender the Jewish people's rights to the land, relinquishing vital, strategic areas to sworn enemies, while trampling on the principles most sacred to the Jewish people throughout the generations. The country is plagued by cultural rifts within its own society along political, religious, and sociological lines, and is morally weakened by a spent nationalist ideology that can no longer inspire its sons and daughters. It is now clear to all that, although millions of Jews have returned to the Promised Land and physically rebuilt it, the State of Israel is very far from fulfilling the Jewish vision of the true and complete redemption.[2]

Nonetheless, "the Holy One, blessed be He, always provides the cure before He inflicts the wound."[3] God has provided the potential to rectify this seemingly hopeless situation. If we examine the workings of Divine Providence, we can discern the cure in the circumstances surrounding the establishment of the state and the liberation of Jerusalem.

HEALING WITH LIGHT

It is surely Divine Providence that the two most outstanding events in the relatively short history of modern Israel both occurred in the month of Iyar. To fully appreciate the significance of this, we must turn to the Torah, God's plan of creation.

We must first consider the name of the month, for God creates everything—both tangible entities and temporal or spiritual phenomena[4]—through its Hebrew name.[5]

The month's common name, *Iyar*, is related to the word for "light," *or*. Indeed, in the Bible, there is one explicit reference to the month of Iyar, and there it is called *Ziv* ("radiance").[6]

In Kabbalah, the word *Iyar* is seen as an acronym for the Hebrew phrase, "I am GOD, your healer."[7] Thus, the month of Iyar is understood to be the month of Divine healing power—healing with light. (This is in accordance with the way of the Ba'al Shem Tov—not to attack darkness directly, head on, but rather to disarm it with light: "a little light dispels much darkness."[8])

A SECOND CHANCE

Why is healing with light particularly relevant to the situation in Israel today? To appreciate this, let us examine the unique place the month of Iyar occupies in the Torah's scheme of time.

In the Torah, only one holiday falls in the month of Iyar: the festival of the Second Passover (*Pesach Sheini*) on the fourteenth day of the month. Normally, the Torah tells us to celebrate Passover on the fourteenth day of Nisan, the month before Iyar. But a person ritually impure or too far away from the Temple on the fourteenth of Nisan—and therefore unable to celebrate Passover by bringing a sacrifice to the Temple on that day—has another chance, the Second Passover.[9]

Although the Jewish year begins in the month of Tishrei, the months are counted from Nisan. Iyar is thus the "second" month both in the ordinal sense and inasmuch as it is the month in which one is given a second chance.

Every holiday in the Jewish calendar teaches us a basic lesson how to fulfill our purpose in life, how to serve God maximally the whole year. The message of the Second Passover—and thus, the general message of the month of Iyar—is that it is never too late.[10] No matter in what situation we find ourselves, no matter how low we have fallen, no matter how impure we may feel or how far away from our life's goal we are, we can always, with God's help, rectify our situation.[11]

And so it is with regard to the State of Israel. The fact that it was founded and its wars were fought and won in the month of Iyar teaches us that we must not despair. The power of light can overcome the darkness; it is never too late to rectify the situation.

LEAPING OVER OBSTACLES

Where can we draw the power necessary to do this? If we compare the resources at our disposal with the forces we must overcome, the obstacles indeed seem insurmountable.

We can take our cue from another significant date in the month of Iyar. The second day of Iyar is celebrated by the Hassidim as the birthday of Rabbi Shmuel of Lubavitch.[12] The Talmudic sages teach us that on a person's birthday, his soul-root (*mazal*) radiates most strongly.[13]

Rabbi Shmuel is identified with his best-known saying: "People generally say that if you are confronted with an obstacle, you should try first to go under it, and only if that fails, try to leap over it. But I say: *lechatchilah ariber*—you should always, as your first option, leap over it."[14]

We are taught in Kabbalah that God created the world in two general stages, referred to as the two "worlds" or "states of being" of Chaos (*Tohu*) and Order (*Tikun*). The world of *Tohu* was a high-energy, chaotic state of being. This state or primordial "world" was unstable and doomed to collapse. The "collapse" of a world implies "the breaking of its vessels" (*shevirat hakeilim*), which leads to a state of existential confusion and concealment of the Creator from His creation. With the collapse of the primordial World of *Tohu* began a process of repair or rectification, a process of reestablishing order—the World of *Tikun*.

God created the world in this fashion for two reasons: (1) in order to give us free choice (by concealing His omnipresence) and (2) in order to simultaneously invest reality with infinite potential (derived from the initial, high-energy state of reality) to advance His plan for creation.

The confusion that resulted from the collapse of the first world serves to conceal God's presence and directing hand, giving us free choice. The high-energy state of the primordial world remains in the present order as "potential energy," endowing us with unlimited power to achieve. Normally, we are not conscious of the high-energy state; this is intentional, for it allows us to devote the conscious faculties of our souls to build rectified "vessels" to contain the "lights" yet to be revealed.

The boldness of spirit necessary to live according to Rabbi Shmuel's instruction, to always leap *over* obstacles as our first, unhesitating option—*lechatchilah ariber*—derives from the great, infinite "lights" of the World of *Tohu*.

The Rebbe, in his address of Nisan 28, 5751 (1991),[15] in preparation for the spiritual service of the month of Iyar, said that the way for us to bring the Messiah is by vesting the intense "lights" of *Tohu* in the mature "vessels" of *Tikun*. Without the lights of *Tohu*, we are powerless to stand up to the challenge of our times, to tackle a world situation in desperate need of salvation, to do all in our power to bring the Messiah now. Without the broad, mature vessels of *Tikun*, we cannot properly integrate and know how to best express to the world the powerful messages and energies of the Messiah.

In the coming chapters, we will attempt to develop a workable model for constructing such vessels. Providing the "intense lights" to fill these vessels is then everyone's individual and collective challenge—both of the Jewish people and of the world. We can meet this challenge by being always ready, as our first option, to leap over obstacles: *lechatchilah ariber*!

RECTIFYING THE HEART

As to *how* we should rectify things, we can again seek inspiration from the significance and uniqueness of the month of Iyar, which is so clearly tied to the destiny of the State of Israel.

Iyar is distinguished by the fact that there is a special commandment that we fulfill on each and every day of the month—the commandment to count the forty-nine days (seven weeks) from Passover to Shavuot (literally, "weeks"), the day when the Torah was given on Mt. Sinai. This time period is known as "the Counting of the Omer," after the "measure [*omer*] of the first of your harvest" offered in the Temple on the second day of Passover.[16]

God delivered the Jewish people from the bondage of Egypt so that they could receive the Torah.[17] We relive the Exodus from Egypt every year on Passover by experiencing how God redeems us from our personal, spiritual bondage; the goal of our yearly redemption is that we receive a new and more sublime revelation of God's Torah on Shavuot, because reaching a higher level of Divine consciousness is the essence of freedom. The entire period of counting the Omer—most of which occurs during Iyar—is thus one of anticipation.[18]

In Kabbalah, we are taught that the path from Passover to Shavuot—from redemption to revelation—is a process of spiritual growth, in which we rectify the seven emotions of the heart. In the immature heart, the emotions are unilateral; each pursues its course of action without considering the other emotions. This chaotic situation must be rectified if the newfound freedom is to be translated into a new, higher vision of reality. To rectify the heart, every emotion must learn to take all its sister-emotions into consideration. This lends balance and harmony both to each individual emotion and to the full emotional array of the heart. Indeed, "balance" is often a synonym for "rectification" in Kabbalah. This process is called "inter-inclusion."[19]

For example, the first two attributes of the heart are the opposite but complementary[20] emotions of love and fear. In order to rectify the attribute of love, we must find and express an element of fear in our experience of love (for example, the fear that the bond of love between ourselves and our beloved might be severed). In order to rectify the attribute of fear (after we have learned to focus our fear solely on God—and on those whom God commands us to fear), we must find and express an element of love in our experience of fear (for example, a love and respect that we show someone we fear or stand in awe of).

The heart possesses seven emotions—love, fear, mercy, confidence, sincerity, devotion, and humility. *Each* of the seven must be taught to identify and experience *all* of the seven. This gives us a total of forty-nine stages of inter-inclusion. On each of the forty-nine days from Passover to Shavuot, as we "count the Omer," we rectify an individual aspect of our emotional makeup.

Counting the Omer begins in Nisan and ends in the month following Iyar, Sivan. But while only half of Nisan (the last fifteen days) and a sixth of Sivan (the first five days) are part of the period of counting the Omer, the entire month of Iyar is devoted to this task. And so, the month of Iyar is specifically identified with this commandment.

Here we see that the month most clearly identified with the rise of the State of Israel is a month of rectification. This means that the State of Israel was created to be rectified, and that the process we must follow in rectifying it is the process of the Omer—the sequential rectification of the seven emotions of the heart.

THE THREE SAGES OF THE MONTH OF IYAR

We are taught in Kabbalah that the rectification of the emotions depends upon the rectification of its antecedents: the intellect and the attributes of the personality that transcend the intellect. The key to rectifying these faculties is also found in the month of Iyar.

Three great Talmudic sages are associated with this month: Rabbi Akiva, Rabbi Shimon bar Yochai, and Rabbi Meir. Rabbi Shimon, Rabbi Meir, and all of Rabbi Akiva's students passed away during this month. We are taught that on the day of a sage's passing (and on the anniversary of this day every year) his life's work reaches its apex (and, on every succeeding year, new heights) and becomes spiritually revealed and accessible to everyone.[21]

Rabbi Shimon's name is derived from the verb "to hear." Rabbi Meir's name is derived from the word for "light," and is thus associated with sight. In Kabbalah, sight and hearing are metaphors for the two basic faculties of the intellect: insight/wisdom (*chochmah*) and understanding (*binah*). Thus, Rabbi Meir and Rabbi Shimon personify *chochmah* and *binah*, respectively. Indeed, the sages comment that Rabbi Meir's name befitted him, because he was so insightful that "he enlightened the eyes of the sages,"[22] and Rabbi Shimon is known as the author of the *Zohar*, the fundamental text of Kabbalah, which enables mortal man to understand the mysteries of creation.[23]

Rabbi Akiva's name comes from the word for "heel." The heel is the lowest part of the person, but, inasmuch as "the end is wedged in the beginning,"[24] it alludes to the highest faculty of the personality, the super-intellect (called in Kabbalah *keter*, the "crown").

Thus, these three sages—the master (Rabbi Akiva) and his two greatest disciples (Rabbi Meir and Rabbi Shimon) personify the super-intellect (*keter*) and the intellect (*chochmah* and *binah*), the antecedents of the emotions.[25]

Significantly, these three sages were the outstanding messianic personalities of their age, in that all three were consumed with the fire of messianic enthusiasm.

Rabbi Akiva's twenty-four thousand students died during the period of the counting of the Omer. According to some, they died in a plague, while others state that they died in Bar Kochba's revolt against the Roman Empire. Rabbi Akiva believed that Bar Kochba was the Messiah and therefore endorsed his leadership and promoted his cause.

In any case, we are taught that Rabbi Akiva's students died because they were guilty of the sin of not honoring one another as they should have done.[26] In connection with this tragedy, Rabbi Akiva taught that the love and respect of one's fellow Jew is the greatest, all-inclusive commandment of the Torah.[27] Encapsulating the entire Torah into this one commandment is a messianic imperative, for we are taught that the Temple was destroyed because of mutual disrespect and groundless hatred.[28] This implies that the Messiah will rebuild it when the Jewish people learn to love and respect one another unqualifiedly.[29]

Rabbi Shimon, as noted, is the author of the *Zohar*, which describes the process whereby we can reunite God with His creation—the goal of the messianic redemption. As Rabbi Shimon states, in order for the Messiah to come in peace and mercy, we must delve into the secrets of the Kabbalah as he revealed them.[30]

Rabbi Shimon passed away on the thirty-third day of the Omer—Lag BaOmer—the eighteenth day of the month of Iyar. This day is therefore[31] referred to as the day of the giving of the inner dimension of the Torah to Israel.

Moreover, Rabbi Shimon asked that we rejoice on Lag BaOmer as we would at a wedding,[32] for, he said, it essentially *was* a wedding: He promised that when he ascended to heaven on this day (and to a higher heavenly realm every year on this day), he would unite the immanent light of God[33] with the transcendent light of God. The immanent light of God is the awareness that although the world does exist, it exists only by virtue of God's energy constantly flowing into it. The transcendent light of God is the awareness that God transcends creation absolutely and that all of creation is nonexistent relative to God's existence. The paradoxical union of these two perspectives—a reality that is simultaneously aware of its own existence yet consummately absorbed in its awareness of God—is the goal of creation. Thus, Rabbi Shimon's promise was a messianic one, for from this "marriage" the spirit of redemption descends (is "born") into reality.

Rabbi Meir passed away on the very day of the Second Passover, the fourteenth of Iyar, the day that teaches us that it is never too late.

Rabbi Meir regarded *himself* as the potential Messiah of his generation.[34] His messianic character was manifest in his lifetime when he miraculously saved people's lives on a number of occasions; because of this he became known as "the master of miracles."[35] He even taught that if someone is in danger, he should cry out, "God of Meir, answer me!" and God will answer him.[36]

Based on this, it has become customary for someone who has lost something to pray, "God of Meir, answer me," in order to invoke the merit of Rabbi Meir in asking God to help him find the lost item. It is indeed appropriate that we should ask God—in Rabbi Meir's merit—to help us find that which is lost, for the day of his passing (when, as we said above, his life's work reached its apex and became accessible to all) is the Second Passover, which teaches us that "it is never too late." In fact, the original Yiddish idiom for the phrase, "it is never too late" is *es iz nito kein farfaln*, "nothing is lost"—there is never a lost cause.

We thus see that the association of these three sages with the month of Iyar implies that in order for the rectification process to succeed, the super-intellect and intellect must be suffused with messianic orientation.[37] Indeed, according to Kabbalah and Hassidic tradition, the month of Iyar—because of the anticipation and rectification associated with its distinctive commandment, the counting of the Omer—is a messianic month, conducive to focusing all of our intentions on the immanent coming of the Messiah.[38]

There are many short-term goals that can serve as immediate motivating factors in the search for solutions. But only the long-term, ultimate goal of messianic redemption can empower a rectification process of the revolutionary proportions needed to solve the problems of the State of Israel. When we infuse our mental and transcendental faculties with messianic orientation, they can drive the ensuing rectification process to its true fulfillment.

CHAPTER TWO

The Path to Light

SHATTERED VESSELS, SHATTERED DREAMS

As we all know, the problems facing the Jewish people in modern-day Israel affect Jews and non-Jews the world over. They have resulted from mistaken attitudes and false ideologies that we must now set straight.[1]

As we mentioned above, our present situation is the result of "the breaking of the vessels" (*shevirat hakeilim*). In the World of *Tohu*, the lights are great while the vessels are small; the "body" of the world has not sufficiently developed and matured to be able to integrate its own lights, like an immature youth unable to integrate his own insights and experiences. The result, in the case of the youth, is psychological breakdown.

The light inherent in the Zionist dream—the aspiration that the Jewish people, after nearly two thousand years of exile, return to their homeland—is indeed great, but its secularly-oriented vessels are small and immature. Secular Zionism has succeeded in creating material vessels, constructing buildings and roads, developing industry, and creating institutions of higher, secular education. But it has willfully neglected, or even rejected, the inner, spiritual dimension of the vessels themselves—the conscious intention that they serve God's purpose in creation.

Without this inner dimension, no matter how great the vessels (physical accomplishments) may seem, they remain immature, unable to contain and integrate the light of the Zionist dream. This is similar to the example of the youth above: physical maturity—a well-developed body—in no way implies the psychological maturity necessary to contain spiritual lights. The result: the very light shatters its own vessels.

Every day, the "vessels" that have been created by the secular Zionist dream—of the Jewish people returning to the Land of Israel and establishing there a safe haven from the perils of the Diaspora in the form of a secular Jewish state, whose ultimate goal is to live in peace and harmony with its Arab neighbors[2]—are shattering before our eyes.

On the one hand, Zionism has succeeded in accomplishing its goal of creating a refuge for the Jewish people, a sovereign, independent state in the Land of Israel. On the other hand, the sad truth is that the predicament we now face is in a certain sense worse than that which we faced before the success of Zionism.

Before Zionism, although Jews were by and large unwanted guests under foreign regimes and lived in continual danger, they nevertheless (for the most part) proudly retained their Jewish identity. Now, we have returned to our homeland and possess a strong and skilled army (despite which, we continue to face grave dangers from our Arab neighbors). Nonetheless, our very identity as Jews—the innate Jewish pride that has kept us alive over the millennia—is in danger. The sociological phenomenon of so-called post-Zionism, even more secular in its orientation than was its predecessor, the original Zionism, threatens to undermine Jewish identity by replacing it with either cosmopolitan identity or an "Israeli" identity, devoid of Judaism.

What is necessary, according to Kabbalah, is that we immediately prepare ourselves to repair[3] these broken vessels, to rectify the State of Israel.

Dreams by nature are unordered and chaotic.[4] In order to transform a dream into reality, its ideas and visions have to be ordered and arranged into a functional hierarchy based on their interrelations and the way they relate to existing reality. In Kabbalah, this is the transition process from *Tohu* to *Tikun*. Kabbalah therefore provides us with the structural framework through which we can organize the disparate elements of the dream of redemption into a viable program to rectify reality. Without this integral and self-consistent order, the Zionist dream is doomed to remain a misty haze of inspired but impossible-to-realize fantasies.

Furthermore, imposing order on the vagueness of the dream enables us to work patiently and methodically toward our ultimate goal. The clear vision of our direction and objective gives us faith that our small initial steps will enable us to gain the momentum and strength to take increasingly larger and quicker steps. In the terminology of Kabbalah, as the vessels of *Tikun* mature, they become capable of containing more and more of the infinite lights of *Tohu*.[5]

Finally, order lends grace and attractiveness to the dream.[6] And when its elements are shown to be a patterned, unified, and practical whole, their intrinsic beauty becomes apparent. Then, it becomes possible to inspire others with the same dream.[7]

That said, the purpose of order is not to straightjacket us into a rigid mode of action that knows no deviations. As with art in general, symmetry and order often serve as the backdrop for the occasional departure that expresses true artistry. In Judaism, this is the difference between the "style" of the Divine service of the *tzadik* (holy person) and that of the *ba'al teshuvah* (one who is returning to God). The *tzadik* progresses from step to step in the service of God in logical, relentless order; the *ba'al teshuvah* progresses in fits and starts, impetuously alternating between symmetric order and asymmetric divergences from logical order.[8]

Before the beginning of a rectification process, an explosive, asymmetric phenomenon is often necessary in order to set things in motion. The crisis that inspired the dream of rectification in the first place must jolt us out of our complacency. After the initial, explosive reaction, the reasoned process of imposing order can ensue.[9]

As we shall see, the ultimate, messianic goal of this process is that we live in our Promised Land serving God in joy, the joy that comes with consummate wholeness—a whole Jewish people living in a whole Land of Israel in full accordance with all the statutes of the Torah. For the present, we must do everything in our power to increase Jewish identity and commitment to the way of the Torah— permeated by messianic awareness and aspiration—the world over. This will enable us to reach a critical mass of Jewish consciousness ready and willing to implement the process to be described.[10]

As we examine the various stages of the process of rectification, we will see how their implementation is up to each and every one of us. We must all illuminate the darkness around us and, ultimately, transform the darkness into light.

TRANSFORMING DARKNESS INTO LIGHT

While, at first glance, the task of repairing the dire situation we find ourselves in today may seem huge, God Himself provided us with the best possible model when He transformed darkness into light on the first day of creation, as the Book of Genesis relates[11]:

> *In the beginning, God created the heavens and the earth. And the earth was void and empty, and darkness was on the face of the abyss, and the spirit of God hovered over the face of the waters. And God said, "Let there be light," and there was light. And God saw that the light was good, and God separated the light from the darkness. And God called the light "day" and the darkness He called "night." And there was evening and there was morning, one day.*

As we see from this account, God created light against the background of primordial darkness. But initially, light was commingled with darkness; rather than pure, clear white, the light appeared gray. As such, light's inherent goodness could not illuminate the world. And so, God separated the light from the darkness. He further defined the parameters of the light and the darkness by giving each a name. Still, this was not God's final goal; God's final goal was union—not separation—of the two distinct entities. When the first day concluded, light and darkness, day and night, evening and morning, were united to become *"one* day."[12]

The Torah's account of the first day of creation alludes to our own ultimate purpose in creation. We begin in the dark, generating light against the background of our own innate state of darkness. However, this light commingles with the darkness, leaving us with confused shades of gray. We must then separate the light from the darkness, giving each its own well-defined domain. Finally, working together with God as partners in consummating the work of creation, we transform the darkness itself into light, so that all of God's creation may shine forth as *"one* day."

According to Kabbalah, the seven days of creation further detail the process by which the primordial darkness becomes fully transformed into light in our consciousness.[13] Each day of creation is a stage of rectification. These stages follow the order of the corresponding seven emotions of the heart, as we will detail further on.

"WHEN I FELL, I AROSE..."

The transformation of darkness into light that we are called upon to accomplish in our generation is alluded to in the Bible. The prophet Micah[14] teaches:

> *When I fell, I arose;*
> *When I dwell in darkness,*
> *GOD is my light.*

The Ba'al Shem Tov teaches that all prophetic messages are relevant to all of us at all times and in all places and that we should strive to understand the words of the Torah as relating to current events.[15] In this vein, this verse may be interpreted as follows:

"When I fell, I arose" alludes to the establishment of the State of Israel, which arose after the greatest fall and tragedy that the Jewish people had ever suffered, the Holocaust.[16]

"When I dwell in darkness" alludes to the fact that even though the State of Israel arose as a gift from God, we nonetheless continue to dwell in spiritual darkness. Recognizing this fact—and making every effort in our power to transform the darkness into light—is the challenge of our generation.

To transform darkness into light, we must be constantly conscious of God's Presence and desire to serve Him in truth and love. Then we become fully aware of God's "light," His constant presence and Providence over every aspect of our lives—"GOD is my light." Inspired by this awareness, we reveal in ourselves untapped resources that will enable us to fully engage in the sacred task of realizing God's desire in creation—to transform the world around us into a dwelling place for the revelation of His infinite light.

For us, then, the words of the prophet Micah transmit the following message: "The last generation was the generation of *When I fell, I arose.* This generation is the generation of *When I dwell in darkness, GOD is my light.*"[17]

THE PATH TO LIGHT

The path to light begins with understanding darkness, for by understanding darkness we gain the power to transform it into light. In Kabbalah, we are taught that this transformation process consists of five successive levels of consciousness, which are manifest in the five ascending levels of the soul:

- First is the initial awareness of the darkness around us. This is the consciousness of the *nefesh* ("created soul"), the lowest level of the soul, which perceives the objective reality of the surrounding world.

- Second is the awareness of our own inner state of darkness. This is the consciousness of the next higher level of the soul, the *ruach* ("spirit"), which relates to the emotions.

- Third is the awareness that the darkness itself possesses an inner, concealed core of potential light. This is the consciousness of the *neshamah* ("breath"), the soul's faculty of in-depth contemplation.

- Fourth is the appearance, within us, of the hidden light. This is the consciousness of the *chayah* ("living being"), the experience of a lightning flash of new insight across the consciousness of the soul.

- Fifth is the experience of the actual transformation of the external darkness into light. This is the consciousness of the *yechidah* ("single one"), the soul's messianic consciousness.

	level of soul		experience	stage of transformation
stage 5	*yechidah*	"single one"	messianic consciousness	transformation of the external darkness into light
stage 4	*chayah*	"living being"	insight	appearance of the hidden light within us
stage 3	*neshamah*	"breath"	in-depth contemplation	awareness that the darkness possesses an inner, concealed core of potential light
stage 2	*ruach*	"spirit"	emotions	awareness of our inner state of darkness
stage 1	*nefesh*	"created soul"	perception of objective reality	awareness of the darkness around us

As applied to the current sociopolitical situation, these five stages are as follows:

• First, we must recognize the darkness of reality—the darkness of the situation we confront—for what it is. Jewish values are despised and the Jewish people are persecuted in much of the world. It is imperative that in wishing it were otherwise we not bury our heads in the sand.

This is possible only if we are not afraid of the darkness—which we should not fear in any case, since, as believing Jews, we should fear only God, the omnipotent and omnipresent One. Empowered by our faith, we become able to relate objectively to the darkness that encompasses us, to come to terms with our present situation, in order to effect a change for the better.

• Second, we must understand that the darkness of the reality outside us reflects our own inner state of darkness. With regard to the founders and leaders of the State of Israel, both past and present[18]—together with us, the public whom they represent and whose consciousness is both forged and reflected by them—this inner darkness has manifested itself primarily as arrogance. The Torah defines arrogance as an attitude that ascribes success and achievement to "*my* power and the strength of *my* hands."[19] This arrogance has blocked the revelation of God's light and so is responsible for all the darkness and evil around us.[20]

But knowing the cause of an illness is already half of its cure. By defining the illness and thus confining it within boundaries, we make room outside for healing light to appear. Sparks of light—that is, the growing awareness that God controls the world, not us, and that by His power alone can we succeed in our endeavors—can now begin to find their way into our consciousness.

This new awareness fosters the hope that our entire reality will eventually be sweetened and illuminated. We have been promised that out of the darkness a great light is destined to shine forth, as the prophet Isaiah foretold: "The people walking in darkness beheld a great light."[21]

In this verse, not only does darkness transform into light, but *while* walking in darkness, the people beheld a *great light*. The entire verse reads: "The people walking in darkness beheld a great light; a light shone on those dwelling in the land of the shadow of death."

How pertinent is this verse for our times! Because we walk in spiritual darkness, we dwell in a land where the shadow of death, in the form of Arab terrorism, threatens us from around. By first transforming our own spiritual darkness into great light we will illuminate, and thereby dismiss, the dark shadow of death threatening us. For if "even a little light dismisses much darkness"—how much more so a great light.

• Next, we must deeply analyze our inner darkness, attempting to identify in its very essence that which is positive and desirable. No evil is totally devoid of good, for if it were so, it could not exist. Continual influx of Divine energy is necessary to sustain everything, even the darkest state of being. Indeed, as the prophet Isaiah implies, in the inner essence of the darkness lies a *great* light; it is just initially concealed by virtue of its profundity.

Often, the inner darkness, seeking to attain public acclaim, will appear in the garb of some positive, universal value. The most significant example of this in our times is the so-called "peace process." The sages have taught us that there is nothing greater than peace,[22] but with regard to the present peace process, how appropriate are the words of the prophet: "They say 'peace, peace,' but there is no peace."[23]

The result of the cry "peace, peace" is actually the very opposite of peace. It is a peace that leads to war and bloodshed. From the words of King Solomon, the wisest of all men, we learn that the general rule is that war—a war fought to reveal God's eternal truth to the world, His plan for the ultimate good of all humanity—is a necessary prerequisite for peace: "There is a time for war, and [then] a time for peace."[24] The war must be fought to the end, not ceased in the middle. Only with the total victory of good over evil can true peace ensue.

Here again, the inner state of darkness that motivates the "peace process" is in essence arrogance and material self-interest. The great light that lies concealed in the inner core of the darkness is the ideal of peace, an ideal which, when not misconstrued, reflects the greatness of God, the "Master of Peace,"[25] in the world which He created for His glory.[26]

Only our faith in the presence of that which we cannot directly sense is able to address this concealed light and goodness. Regarding the inner darkness of arrogance itself, we must believe that the false and harmful sense of personal/national greatness we have described is in essence a fallen, perverted expression of positive pride. The only positive pride is: "Pride and greatness belong to the Life of all Worlds."[27] It is only befitting of God, the "Life of all Worlds," to take pride in His deeds (for in taking pride, as it were, He reveals His greatness to humanity). With strong and perfect faith, we can begin to fathom the Divine greatness present in its distorted representation.

- Then, the essential light inherent in the darkness that we have known now only through faith will begin to manifest and take form as an inner light shining within us. God's own greatness—and the pride He takes in His people Israel—will begin to fill our hearts with a deep sense of Jewish pride, the pride of the one chosen by God to bear the torch of true peace to the whole world. Guided by the beacon and power source of Divine energy, we will be able to stand up and act to change the world for the better.[28]

- Finally, this inner light will shine from within us, impressing itself upon reality and changing reality.[29] By transforming internal, spiritual darkness into light, we will, by the grace of God, transform external, material darkness into light as well. The world will acknowledge the greatness of God, His Torah, and His people, and join us in joyfully crowing Him as King over all the earth. We will then have succeeded in making a full turn—from the sense of darkness surrounding and threatening our very existence to the full revelation of God's infinite light encompassing us and permeating our consciousness, our physical being, and everything around us.

	soul	experience	stage of transformation	present situation
stage 5	*yechidah* "single one"	messianic consciousness	transformation of the external darkness into light	universal acknowledgment of the greatness of God
stage 4	*chayah* "living being"	insight	appearance of the hidden light within us	Jewish pride
stage 3	*neshamah* "breath"	in-depth contemplation	awareness that the darkness possesses an inner, concealed core of potential light	awareness that our arrogance is a fallen state of God's greatness
stage 2	*ruach* "spirit"	emotions	awareness of our inner state of darkness	we and our leaders are arrogant
stage 1	*nefesh* "created soul"	perception of objective reality	awareness of the darkness around us	Jewish values are despised and the Jewish people are persecuted

MAKING THEORY FIT REALITY

The process of rectification that we will present, while based on the ancient teachings of the Kabbalah, takes modern society as it is into full consideration. As is true of any living organism, the Torah in general and its inner soul, Kabbalah, in particular, grows and develops with the times, always adjusting itself to current reality. In this adjustment process, nothing essential is changed; rather, new, concealed dimensions are revealed. Kabbalah is always old and new simultaneously. When properly understood and implemented with conviction and devotion, the theory outlined in Kabbalah really works in the world.

Kabbalah teaches that in order to effect a positive change in the world around us, the Divine plan or "theory"[30] must meet and mate with reality—with human consciousness, expressed in the opinions and value systems of the times.[31]

Both the consciousness of "heaven" and the consciousness of "earth" were created by God in accordance with His Divine blueprint of reality—the words of the Torah. Since the words of the Torah cast and structure all reality, it is never necessary to compromise them for the sake of addressing reality. Deep down in its unconscious core, reality knows that the Torah is its source and that without the Torah it cannot exist.[32]

In order for us to help bring about the rectification of reality as God envisions it in the Torah, we must know how to make the eternal values of the Torah fit reality as it exists in the present. This is primarily the task of the oral tradition of the Torah,[33] as revealed by the sages of each generation.[34]

Kabbalah further teaches that any process of rectification proceeds according to the order of the channels of Divine energy through which God created the world—known as the *sefirot* (supernal "lights" or "channels of Divine creative power"). These are:

	expression		inner experience	
superconscious powers	*keter*	crown	*emunah*	faith
			ta'anug	pleasure
			ratzon	will
intellectual faculties	*chochmah*	wisdom	*bitul*	selflessness
	binah	understanding	*simchah*	joy
	da'at	knowledge	*yichud*	union
emotional attributes	*chesed*	loving-kindness	*ahavah*	love
	gevurah	might	*yirah*	fear
	tiferet	beauty	*rachamim*	mercy
	netzach	victory	*bitachon*	confidence
	hod	splendor	*temimut*	sincerity
	yesod	foundation	*emet*	devotion
	malchut	kingdom	*shiflut*	humility

In addressing the current situation of the State of Israel, and in seeking to illuminate the "darkness that covers the earth,"[35] we must think in terms of stages of rectification paralleling the system of these *sefirot*.

Thus, our examination of the progressive stages necessary for the complete rectification of the State of Israel is ordered in accordance with the division of the *sefirot*, which also correspond to the spiritual powers innate in the soul. They are grouped into three general categories: the three super-conscious powers of the soul; the three intellectual faculties of the soul; and the seven emotive/active attributes of the soul, which are also known as the seven emotions of the heart, as noted earlier. These seven emotions correspond to the seven days of creation, the process through which the primordial darkness is transformed into light:

day/stage	emotions of the heart
one	loving-kindness *(chesed)*
two	might *(gevurah)*
three	beauty *(tiferet)*
four	victory *(netzach)*
five	splendor *(hod)*
six	foundation *(yesod)*
seven	kingdom *(malchut)*

We will first address the motivation necessary to begin the process of rectification—that is, the spiritual powers that guide the rectification and generate within us the will to arise and act. These powers belong to the soul's super-consciousness (its "crown," or *keter*). We will then address the "mind" of the rectification—the clear intellectual assumptions on which the rectification is predicated and which we must internalize for the process to proceed smoothly. The final and major portion of our discussion will address the seven emotions of the heart, the emotive/active stages of our practical platform to establish in our Homeland a rectified Jewish state.

PART TWO

The Source of Rectification

כתר עליון איהו כתר מלכות

The supreme crown is the crown of kingdom

—*Tikunei Zohar*, introduction

CHAPTER THREE

Keter: The Source
of Rectification

SPIRITUAL MOTIVATION

The first supernal light, *keter* ("crown"), corresponds in Kabbalah to the super-conscious level of the soul that crowns, so to speak, the head (that is, the conscious intellect) and governs all of our conscious functioning. This level of super-consciousness—existing beyond the mind (which orchestrates our plans for rectification) and beyond the body (which implements them)—is what provides the spiritual motives that construct the foundation for rectification. Although we may not be aware of these spiritual motives during the planning and implementation stages, they hover above at all times, empowering, animating, and rejuvenating the entire process.

The super-consciousness comprises three spiritual forces (or, in the terminology of the Kabbalah, three "super-heads" of the "crown"):

- *emunah* ("faith"),
- *ta'anug* ("pleasure"), and
- *ratzon* ("will").

Let us explain the manifestation of these forces in relation to the subject at hand—our proposed political platform for the rectification of the State of Israel.

FAITH

The initial shift of orientation in Jewish consciousness toward rectification depends on strengthening our faith. Jews are believers by nature,[1] believing in God and His Torah and faithfully awaiting the Messiah, who will bring complete, Divine redemption to the whole world. All Jews must also believe that they individually hold the key to redemption—for every Jew contains a spark of the Messiah,[2] and each must strive to actualize that spark and, by doing so, rectify reality.

Faith implies the rejection of despair; it is the conviction that "no cause is lost," and, consequently, "if you believe you can damage, believe you can repair."[3] Even though we fully recognize the damage that has been caused by the lack of faith and arrogant spirit of the political leaders of the State of Israel, we can nonetheless be encouraged by contemplating the truth embodied in the words of the sages: "Goodness [always] exceeds evil."[4] Goodness repairs what evil breaks. If we have damaged reality, we can always arise and repair what we ourselves have broken.

Thus, we see that faith is the most powerful force of the soul. In it lies the power to rectify everything. Faith, manifest as devotion, is the power and source of motivation to dedicate our lives to the cause we believe in. Those who possess true and absolute faith are always ready to sacrifice their lives for that in which they believe.

The essence of our faith in the Messiah is itself one with the spark of the Messiah latent in our souls. When a sufficient number of these sparks become revealed in individual Jews, they will join to confer on the Jewish community at large the consciousness of our sacred duty to do everything in our power to correct the current situation.

PLEASURE

After strengthening our faith in God and in His promise of redemption—knowing that we ourselves possess the God-given power to rectify reality—we come to experience a sublime pleasure, a foretaste of the pleasure of the redemption to come. Faith has given us devotion, dedication to our cause. With devotion comes trust and with trust comes a deep sense of satisfaction, as though we have already reached our goal, even before we depart upon the journey ahead of us.

In Kabbalah, we are taught that "there is no goodness higher than pleasure."[5] Pleasure is the highest experience of the soul, which lifts us above all the obstacles (whether virtual, imaginary, or real) that may block our way. Sensing how great and wonderful is the desired state of rectification—a state of Divine good, of "love of delight"[6]—we become uplifted, revealing untapped sources of energy from within.

This experience of pleasure is essential in envisioning a rectified existence and aspiring to it. In faith, we firmly believe that what seems impossible is indeed possible. Faith *makes* the impossible possible. Now, having entered the second super-conscious realm of the soul, pleasure, we begin to taste the sweetness inherent in this possibility: the possible begins to tantalize our inner senses, take form, and actualize in our souls.[7]

WILL

The third super-conscious power of the soul, will, is the existential drive of the soul to project its inner taste of fulfillment and actualization onto the screen of external reality.

Envisioning and delighting in the desired good arouses the will to bring about that good and do so immediately.

Faith alone in the ultimate redemption does not demand that the redemption be immediate. The power of faith in the soul is in essence above time. From the vantage point of pure and simple faith, the redemption is already here if we truly believe in it. How long it will take for the process to unfold itself and manifest in this world is an unknown. It may well be a long-term process; it need not be immediate. In the words of the prophet: "He who believes does not hasten."[8]

But when there is a clear recognition and an actual foretaste of how good the redemption will be—how the complete rectification of the Jewish state and the era of redemption it will usher in is truly "good for the Jews [and the entire world]," how it is an enticing, attractive, delightful, and *achievable* reality—the will to create that reality *here and now* is aroused.

When we sense how good the redemption will be—that there will no longer be any suffering, for everyone will enjoy an unbounded state of both material and spiritual prosperity[9]—we are bound to ask: "Why wait even one moment? Let us get up and do everything in our power to attain this good, now!" Will-power is the direct and substantive source of all rectification strategies. It makes us roll up our sleeves and begin to work hard to achieve our goal.[10]

Of will it is said: "Nothing stands in the face of will."[11] Pleasure lifts us above the obstacles that stand in our way and raises us to a place where the obstacles cease to exist. Will breaks through obstacles and breaks down barriers. Nothing can stand in the way of the power of will and prevent it from reaching its goal.

In envisioning the final redemption, the will of the collective soul of the Jewish people focuses in particular on the Messiah, the king that will make our dreams of redemption come true. We want the Messiah to come now, to redeem the world now.

To be sure, the irrational impetuosity of the will must be channeled through the rationality of the intellect. Otherwise, it is impossible to implement the rationally-ordered stages of rectification that follow.

But, at the same time, it is necessary to manifest the full power of the will, including its inspired focus on the end of the process. Throughout the entire rectification process to be outlined, the Messiah and the rectified Jewish state, the Kingdom of Israel, must remain in the forefront of our consciousness.

Then, we can proceed rationally to do all in our power to implement the plan that will achieve our goal.

PART THREE

The Mind of
Rectification

בחכמה יבנה בית ובתבונה יתכונן
ובדעת חדרים ימלאו

The house shall be built with wisdom,
founded with understanding,
and with knowledge will its rooms be filled.

—Proverbs 24:3-4

CHAPTER FOUR

The Clarification
of the Intellect

CLEAR PERCEPTION

Once *keter*, our super-conscious "crown," propels us to arise and act to rectify our situation, we turn to our intellectual faculties to define a plan of action and give it structure. However, to do so, we must have intellectual clarity. Only when intellectual clarity guides our strides toward rectification can we actually begin to advance toward our goal.

According to Kabbalah, there are three stages of intellectual perception, each corresponding to one of the three faculties of the mind. These three stages culminate in the clarified ability of the intellect to guide our practical actions. Before we examine these stages and the intellectual clarity each provides with regard to the rectification of the State of Israel, we will first look at the relationship between the intellectual faculties of the mind and the role they play in defining the logic necessary to pursue our goal.

In the terminology of Kabbalah, the three intellectual faculties of the mind are:

- *chochmah* ("wisdom"),

- *binah* ("understanding"), and

- *da'at* ("knowledge").

"FATHER" AND "MOTHER" IN THE SOUL

To concretize the way in which these intellectual faculties give rise to actual stages of rectification, Kabbalah refers to *chochmah* and *binah* as father and mother, while *da'at* symbolizes the power of the union between them—a union whose offspring are the emotions of the heart that nourish practical methods of action.

The verse in Proverbs, "Hear, my son, the ethic of your father, and do not forsake the teaching of your mother,"[1] sheds light on the meaning of the father and mother principles. We are taught that "the ethic of your father" refers to the Written Torah and "the teaching of your mother" to the Oral Torah.[2] In the Written Torah, the commandments—the statements of God's will and His directives to humanity—are extremely brief. Each commandment as recorded in the Written Torah requires elucidation by the Oral Torah, in some cases, via entire tractates. The text of the Written Torah hides all the details— just as one drop of a father's semen conceals an entire genetic code. Only the elucidation of these words via the Oral Torah fully reveals God's will—just as gestation within the mother's womb for nine months fleshes out the encoded genes into a full-bodied infant possessing a complete range of highly sophisticated characteristics.

In our case, a seminal idea, a point of *chochmah*, flashes across the mind and illuminates where and how reality must be rectified. From this conceptual seed, all the details of the plan of rectification must develop: generalities must take shape as specifics, and ways of actualizing the fundamental idea of rectification must be crystallized. At the stage of *binah*, we begin to achieve a real, tangible picture of the whole body of national rectification, with a detailed depiction of all of its parts—a complete picture of the optimal Jewish state.[3]

After the first seminal flash and its development into its full array of details comes the faculty of *da'at*—the spiritual faculty that links intellect to action. From the logic guiding the process of rectification, we then move to "the seven days of creation"—the seven emotions of the heart that are born of a clarified intellect and that create reality. In this process, the faculty of *da'at* continues all the while to extract practical rectifications from the intellect and to continually connect our will and insight to our emotions and actions.

COMMITMENT TO THE TRUTH

As we will see, the seminal insight of *chochmah* is the awareness that the rectification process must conform to the directives of the Torah, while *binah* defines for us the details and parameters of how it is to proceed, namely, that rectification can take place only in the context of wholeness and completion, with the clear, unequivocal conviction that God gave the *whole* Land of Israel to the *whole* Jewish people, whose continued presence in their homeland is ensured only by virtue of communal commitment (as in the time that the Jewish people first entered the Land of Israel) to live in accordance with the *whole* Torah.[4]

Finally, *da'at* is the seat of free choice in the soul, where decisions are made—particularly with regard to choosing and marrying one's predestined soul-mate (deciding to differentiate the one from the many). *Da'at* clarifies the essential differences between Jew and non-Jew, between the Land of Israel and all other lands, and between the Divine wisdom of the Torah and all other wisdoms. *Da'at* is the bridge between the intellect and the emotions, between the mind and the heart. Here, one feels the intensity of things "making a difference." Not all are the same; in each group of similar entities only one is to be chosen.

In common parlance, the soul's conscious, intellectual faculty of *chochmah* is committed to "tell the truth"[5]; *binah*, "the *whole* truth"; *da'at*, "nothing but the truth."

We will now examine in more detail each one of the three intellectual faculties of the soul and how these powers pave the way by setting right our outlook on reality and preparing us to enact the seven practical steps of rectification to follow.

CHAPTER FIVE

Chochmah:
Exclusive Authority

THE FIRST FLASH OF INSIGHT

Of *chochmah*, the "father"-principle, it is said, "Hear, my son, the ethic of your father"[1] (as noted above). For the son, the father symbolizes the ultimate source of authority. It is the *chochmah* innate in the Divine soul of Israel that senses that indeed there exists an absolute source of authority, the Torah, and that it must be honored, just as a son is commanded to honor his father.[2] Deep in the psyche of the son is his desire to know and relate to the source of his being within his father's mind,[3] and this he achieves by commitment and devotion to fulfill his father's word, to obey his directives.

The deep, axiom-like recognition of truth characteristic of *chochmah* is described in Kabbalah, metaphorically, as a lightning bolt flashing across the mind. This startling, eureka experience is the insight that there does indeed exist one, absolute truth—the truth of the Torah given by God to His people Israel at Mt. Sinai. Together with the experience of truth comes a deep, intuitive sensation of the infinite goodness and spiritual reward that results from faithful obedience to the word of God. This in turn gives rise

51

in the soul to a state of longing to be told, by the Torah, what to do.[4]

As far as the rectification of the State of Israel is concerned, the initial seed of rectification that we must plant in our consciousness is the recognition of the true and sole source of authority from which all the directives of national rectification will issue, the Torah.

When the question arises, "Who is the supreme authority concerning our way of life?" the faculty of *chochmah* innate to the Jewish soul perceives the answer clearly—the Torah is the ultimate and only source of authority for the Jewish people. The Torah issues from Divine *chochmah*,[5] which, when reflected in the *chochmah* of our Divine soul, provides us with the insight that the words of the Torah are indeed the words spoken to us by our Father in Heaven and thus are the true and sole authority with regard to all aspects of our lives.

WHOM TO OBEY

Beyond the clarity that the Torah is our ultimate source of authority and that every step toward national rectification must stem from the Torah and lead to the full realization of the way of life outlined in it, this clarity of mind has immediate significance. What do those who are presently living in the unrectified State of Israel do in cases where the directives of the Torah contradict the law of the land?

It is obvious that when Israeli law does not clash with Torah law, the former should be obeyed, for it is the law of the land, established for the protection and well being of its citizens. But when they conflict, we must ask the question: "Who is to be obeyed? Who is the real father?"

The answer to this question is couched in a well-known saying of the sages that when a teacher's words differ from a student's, one must obey the teacher.[6] In this saying, the "teacher" refers to God while the "student" refers to any created being. The implication, of course, is that it is the teacher that knows best, and so it is the teacher's word that is to be followed.

Civil disobedience, non-violent protest against social or political wrongs is recognized, legitimate, and even praiseworthy in most enlightened countries around the world. How much more so should it be for Torah-observant Jews in Israel, when it is the Torah itself that demands, in cases of conflict, that one disobey the law of the land in order to obey the law of God.

If soldiers in the Israel Defense Forces are commanded to uproot Jewish settlements in the Land of Israel, the order must be disobeyed. If soldiers or civilians are ordered not to shoot first in self-defense, the order must be disobeyed.

When we realize with complete clarity that our exclusive source of authority—the only father and teacher of the souls of Israel, the father of our Jewish national heritage—is the Torah, we will follow the Torah rather than the laws of the land when the two conflict. Of course, in addition to abiding by the laws of the Torah, we will strive to amend and adjust the laws of the state to coincide with the Torah viewpoint;[7] the implementation of this begins in the third stage of the rectification process. (As noted earlier, making the Torah fit reality is the task of the true Torah sages of the generation.[8])

This initial clarity of *chochmah* requires daring. Right from the start, national rectification demands deviation from the "rules of the game." It demands a new, definitive source of authority, different from that recognized today, which must be honored and obeyed in building a rectified society. Indeed, of *chochmah* it is said, "Wisdom emboldens the wise."[9] Clear recognition of truth empowers one to act without fear of unwarranted criticism.[10] Ultimately, the possessors of Divine wisdom will succeed in changing by the sheer brilliance of their minds—and without any need for compulsion—the attitudes of naysayers.

CHAPTER SIX

Binah: Wholeness

THE TORAH, THE NATION, AND THE LAND

We have seen that the faculty of *chochmah* in the soul manifests itself as the clarity of mind that the Torah is our supreme and exclusive authority. This is the soul's seminal state of clarity, associated with the father principle. In contrast, *binah*, the mother principle, is primarily concerned with the details that develop from the seminal idea. With *binah* comes the awareness that the general needs the specific—that every general principle, once stated as a seminal idea, requires the unfolding of the full multiplicity of details included within it, without which it cannot continue to exist. As is the innate nature of a mother's womb, *binah* recognizes that every limb and cell of the body must develop in full.

In our context, clarity of *binah* means our profound awareness of the necessity that all be whole and complete:[1]

- the Torah,

- the Nation of Israel, and

- the Land of Israel.

The Torah

While *chochmah* perceives the Torah to be our exclusive source of authority, *binah* teaches that even one missing or imperfect letter in a Torah scroll invalidates the whole. This also means that we cannot learn Torah piecemeal, dealing only with certain parts and ignoring others. Furthermore, Jews—to whom it is clear that the general principle is whole only in its full array of details—know that complete observance of the Torah's commandments is achieved only within the entire tapestry of life, private and public. Accordingly, *binah* motivates us to observe all the commandments of the Torah, together with all the customs that have been adopted by the Jewish people over the generations, for they are one, whole living organism. All ultimately derive from the Torah given to Moses at Mt. Sinai.[2]

The Nation

Had even one Jew been missing at the time of the giving of the Torah, we would not have been privileged to receive it. A mother nurtures all of her children individually. Every child must be whole and healthy in order for the family, as a fully integrated unit, to be complete. No individual is expendable.

Furthermore, *binah* teaches us that "no lost soul will remain lost"[3]—that all the Children of Israel will return to God and His Torah and serve Him in the Promised Land, and that all will become partners in the process of national rectification. The entire people will be involved in creating a rectified and upright state; all Jews the world over will identify with the Jewish state in the Jewish homeland. This involvement will, of course, encourage immigration (*aliyah*), as we will discuss further on.

"No lost soul will remain lost" refers as well to the souls of righteous converts, who, as we are taught in Kabbalah, are potentially Jews from the moment they are born. Before the coming of the Messiah, all of these lost souls must return to the fold. The difference between such a lost soul and a lost soul of one born Jewish is that the former must undergo a process of halachic conversion. No matter to what extent the latter has assimilated, his essential identity remains forever that of a Jew. He need not undergo conversion, only be aroused to return to God and His Torah. The former, however, though always having possessed an unconscious affinity to Judaism, must undergo a change of identity—must formally become Jewish through conversion.

Here, we witness the dependency of the wholeness of the people on the wholeness of the Torah. If the conversion is not performed in exact accordance with the dictates of Jewish law, it is to no avail.

Today, one of the greatest crises that face the Jewish people is the infiltration of non-Jews professing to be Jews (having undergone non-halachic conversion or not having undergone conversion at all). (If such would-be converts are not inspired—sometimes at a later stage in their lives—to accept Jewish tradition in full and convert according to Jewish law, it indicates retroactively that they are not of the lost souls that always were potential Jews.) This form of assimilation endangers the integrity of the Jewish people, and, as the Rebbe repeatedly said, physically endangers the lives of Jews in Israel (creating a fifth column in the army and other avenues of communal life). When speaking of "the wholeness of the people," the Rebbe referred in particular to the issue of halachic conversion.

The Land

Binah teaches us that every square inch within the historic borders of the country—the land given by God to Israel, whose borders are well defined in the Torah[4]—is an integral part of it. The sanctity of the Land of Israel is absolute and all-encompassing and is upheld only when all its components are united. A blow to any particular part is a blow to the whole. The whole Land of Israel belongs exclusively to the whole Nation of Israel. Every Jew, including those living presently in the Diaspora, possesses a portion of the Land of Israel. As God gave the whole land to His children Israel as an eternal heritage, giving autonomy to a foreign nation within its borders is inconceivable. And, we may give none of it away.

THREE GOOD REASONS

For three reasons, no part of the Land of Israel presently in our hands may be given away:

At the most practical, pragmatic level, the security risk of giving any part of our land to our enemies makes even the thought of so doing out of the question; doing this would surely endanger the lives of millions of Jews living in Israel. The Rebbe repeatedly emphasized that from the pure vantage point of Jewish law,[5] *this* is the reason that makes giving away any part of the land presently in our possession forbidden.[6] The Rebbe said that if giving away land would save lives (as some argue), then the other two, more spiritual reasons for holding on to all the territories of Israel in our hands would be overridden.[7] But the Rebbe was so sure that giving away land *endangers* Jewish life that he unequivocally declared it forbidden. In his own words: "I am completely and unequivocally opposed to the surrender of any of the liberated areas currently under negotiation...."[8]

At the ethical, emotional level, giving away a gift is a slap in the face of the giver.[9] In our generation, God has given major parts of the Promised Land to His chosen people, through great miracles. What a lack of appreciation we show if we even consider giving it away!

Finally, at the purely intellectual level, the faculty of *binah* teaches us that the Land of Israel must remain complete, just because its identity as the Promised Land demands its wholeness. To voluntarily blemish its integral unity and wholeness is equivalent to blemishing the integral wholeness of the Torah and the integral wholeness of the people.

For this reason, the Torah forbids allowing non-Jews—with the exception of righteous gentiles who are truly at peace with the Jewish people and accept the authority of the Torah—to reside in the Land of Israel.[10] When non-Jews purchase land and live in Israel, they claim rights to the possession of the land, and by so blemishing the integral wholeness of the land, they become a spiritual as well as physical menace to the Jewish people. (On the spiritual plane, their presence acts as a negative influence, arousing in the hearts of the Jewish people—whether consciously or unconsciously—a desire to mingle and assimilate with them.)

The Torah, the Nation of Israel, and the Land of Israel are—and must ever remain—whole, for their intrinsic wholeness derives from a spiritual, Divine source above time. Because they are absolutely and eternally whole in their spiritual source, they must remain whole below, in physical reality. This is the perspective of the rectified mind (in general, and the intellectual faculty of *binah* in particular), which sees things in their source, above the parameters of physical time and space.

In his many talks regarding current events and political issues pertaining to the Land of Israel, the Rebbe related to each one of the three reasons that makes giving away land inconceivable:[11]

When emphasizing the security risks, he said that we must follow the advice of military experts, and not the opinions of politicians or military experts speaking from political perspectives.

When speaking of the miracles by which God restored the land of Israel to us in our times, the Rebbe taught us to believe with a perfect heart that as God is the ultimate good, all that He does is for our good. We must learn to value His most benevolent gift to us and express our gratitude to Him.[12] The Rebbe said that it is the arrogant spirit of "*my* power and the strength of *my* hands," described above, that blinds us from recognizing and appreciating God's gift to us.

But whenever the Rebbe spoke of "the wholeness of the land" (*shleimut ha'aretz*), comparing it to "the wholeness of the Torah" and "the wholeness of the nation," he simply meant that the Land of Israel must remain whole. No part of it may be given away, for in truth, in its source above it always was, is, and will be whole and complete.[13]

SHALOM

In Hebrew, the word for "peace" (*shalom*) comes from the root meaning "whole" (*shalem*).[14] Sadly, those who are responsible for casting political policy and who make the decisions in modern-day Israel do not understand this simple linguistic relationship. The native tongue of the policy makers is Hebrew, but they do not understand the simple implication of the language, that peace depends on wholeness. (Or, if they do understand the relationship theoretically, they do not take it to heart; when it comes to practical application, they consciously repress and disregard it.)

But today, there is no more misconceived and misused term than this. Judaism has given the world the value of peace. The Torah, which teaches that there is nothing greater than peace,[15] was given to make peace "above, in the higher worlds, and below, on earth."[16] The whole world knows that Jews greet one another with the word "peace"—*Shalom*—and that this is the way that all peoples should greet and relate to one another.[17]

Of the present misconstrued talk of peace (e.g., "land for peace") the prophet cries, "They say 'peace, peace,' but there is no peace!"[18] Peace will *never* come by relinquishing wholeness. Peace *will* come when we learn to recognize the value of wholeness.

In Kabbalah, we learn that in order for the sense of wholeness to give birth to peace (in the heart and flesh of humanity), the boldness of *chochmah*, the father principle, must unite with the wholeness of *binah*, the mother principle—that is, an augmented influx of energy must flow from father to mother.

The boldness necessary to bring peace demands that the Jew stand up and boldly proclaim to everyone that God has given the whole Land of Israel to His people Israel.[19]

This is unlike the present reality in Israel, whose Jewish leaders—together with their chronic affliction of arrogance, described above—suffer from a deeply-engrained inferiority complex *vis-à-vis* their Jewishness in the face of the non-Jewish world. (In Kabbalah and Hassidism, we are taught that the arrogance that comes with forgetting God[20] and feelings of inferiority toward the non-Jewish world are in fact two sides of the same coin.) By making their sense of inferiority known to the non-Jew, Jewish leaders give legitimacy to the non-Jew's claim to the Land of Israel. Without their encouragement, our enemy would be powerless.[21]

In addition, because of this inferiority complex, we are over-grateful to our allies (in particular, to the United States) for their financial and military assistance to us. We make ourselves forget that "all that the nations do is for their own interests"[22] and that for every plane they give Israel, three are given to our Arab neighbors.[23]

With regard to the United States in particular—which, relative to the other world powers, is definitely benevolent (a *malchut chesed*), as the Rebbe often said—we forget that it pursues a policy of keeping Israel dependent upon it, constraining Israel's progress toward military and economic self-sufficiency. It also does not allow Israel a complete victory over its Arab enemies. In the past, it persistently allowed Israel to win its wars militarily while forcing it to lose them politically. Now, it denies Israel even military victory.

Psychologically, this policy of repression stems from the non-Jewish (both Christian and Moslem) conscious or unconscious fear that Jewish success or victory will signal the fulfillment of the Torah's messianic prophecies, which will invalidate non-Jewish expectations concerning the End of Days.

With affirmativeness and boldness, the Jew will win the respect of the non-Jew, who will honor and acknowledge the truth of the words of the Bible spoken by the Jew. Together, boldness and a sense of wholeness will bring true and lasting peace to Israel and to the world.[24] This is the meaning of the verse,[25] "GOD gives His people boldness, GOD blesses His people with peace."[26]

In summation: *Binah* is the recognition that as long as there is no comprehensive outlook encompassing every detail, the bond between the people, the land, and the Torah is incomplete. The intrinsic wholeness of the Jewish enterprise is actualized via each and every one of its components. None can be compromised.

CHAPTER SEVEN

Da'at:
The Distinctiveness of Israel

TWO SIDES: RIGHT AND LEFT

The intellectual faculties of *chochmah* and *binah* have established that the Torah is our exclusive source of authority and that wholeness must be sought in all matters essential to the state—observance of the entire Torah by the entire Jewish people throughout the entire Land of Israel. The faculty of *da'at* is the concentrated focus of the mind that connects it to the emotions of the heart[1]—the attributes of the soul that correspond to the actual steps of rectification in the process to be described.

In Kabbalah, *da'at* possesses two sides: Its right side is the knowledge or recognition of that which is good, accompanied by a sense of magnetic-like attraction toward the good. Its left side is the knowledge or recognition of that which is evil, accompanied by a sense of repulsion from the evil. These two sides of *da'at* are alluded to by the primordial Tree of Knowledge of Good and Evil.[2]

In greater depth, the negative or repellant force inherent in the soul's intellectual faculty of *da'at* is its ability to distinguish between good and evil, to prevent the good and the evil from intermingling, to prevent the evil from polluting the good. The positive or attractive force inherent in *da'at* is its ability to convert the inner core of the evil into good for the sake of uniting the innate good and the newly converted state of good[3] to bring into reality new, blessed offspring.

At this point in our discussion, we will only relate to the left (negative/repellant) side of *da'at*, its ability to separate, for this is what sets the mind straight so it can begin the actual rectification process,[4] whose first five steps are based on the principle of "separation." Only when reaching the sixth step—the union of Torah and science (the higher waters of creation reaching down to the lower waters and the lower waters reaching up to the higher waters)—does the power inherent in the right side of *da'at* come to the fore.[5]

Da'at distinguishes between good and evil within reality. In the words of the sages: "Without knowledge, how can one make distinctions?"[6] Differentiation—"between holy and mundane, between light and darkness, between Israel and the nations"[7]—is essential for the practical rectification and refinement of reality. Without differentiation between light and darkness, we can have no correct orientation toward rectification, and therefore there is no actual possibility of change—everything remains theoretical.

As noted earlier, the rectified mind has to clearly distinguish both between the Divine truth embodied in the Torah and in all other wisdoms and between the intrinsic sanctity of the Land of Israel and of all other lands. But first, the distinction must be made between the Jewish people and all other nations, for although our ultimate goal is the rectification of the entire world so that all nations serve God together, the rectification of all humanity depends first upon our and the world's recognition of the essential difference between Jew and non-Jew.

THE CHOSEN PEOPLE

We must make it clear to ourselves and try our best to make it clear to the world around us that the Jewish people has been chosen by God to be a torch-bearer to the nations, to be "a kingdom of priests,"[8] whose purpose is to enlighten and bestow good upon all of humanity. Only when it becomes perfectly clear that in the Divine plan for the rectification of reality the Jew has been chosen to be the spiritual giver to humanity can true rectification begin.[9]

Recognizing what has been chosen by God—from amongst others that closely resemble it—is a function of the intellectual faculty of *da'at*, for indeed the very power of free choice is seated in *da'at*, since it is the mind's power to choose that recognizes something or someone as being chosen. Here the soul knows or senses directly, and confirms the fact that is explicitly and repeatedly stated in the Torah—that the Jewish people has been chosen from all nations and that the Land of Israel has been chosen from all lands. God has given the chosen land to the chosen people as an eternal inheritance. And so, as stated previously, the Land of Israel belongs to all of the Nation of Israel, to each and every Jew, whether living in Israel or in the Diaspora and no one has the authority to give it away.[10]

The practical rectification of the State of Israel depends upon first knowing, with complete clarity and certainty, that the Jewish people is indeed God's chosen people and is characterized as the giver. And the very characteristic of giving depends on the faculty of *da'at*, as is explained in Kabbalah.

The *Zohar* teaches that the most essential difference between Jew and non-Jew lies in the Jew's power of *da'at*. A Jew possesses "potent" *da'at*, the knowledge characteristic of a giver in essence. The *da'at* inherent in the soul of every Jew allows him or her to "bear fruit" in reality, to give a real and lasting gift. Only by first distinguishing between good and evil and ultimately knowing how to convert evil into good does one manifest his latent potency to give in truth.

Jews who lack the faculty of discernment and imagine that superficial equality prevails throughout reality— beginning with equality between Jew and non-Jew—are flawed in their *da'at*, in their essential Jewish uniqueness.[11] They will be unable to impact reality meaningfully.

The power to discern the essential difference between Jew and non-Jew is unique to the faculty of *da'at* innate in the Jewish soul. Still, it is the Jewish duty to explain this distinction to the non-Jewish world as well.

FRIEND AND FOE

Although the sublime sensitivity to the difference between Jew and non-Jew exists only in the Jewish soul, a more external sense of discernment exists in all human souls (and to a greater or lesser extent, in the souls of all living creatures): the ability to distinguish between friend and foe.[12]

Remarkably, we find in the Bible that Jewish rulers who should have *known* better were often unable—or perhaps, unwilling, blinded by their passion to find favor in the eyes of the non-Jewish world—to distinguish between friend and foe!

The same is true in particular with regard to the majority of Israeli politicians and policy makers.[13] Their external faculty of *da'at* has been so numbed that they see sworn enemies as potential allies and friends. In expressing mercy to enemies and making peace treaties with them, believing them to be friends, they become cruel to their own people, their true friends. In the words of our sages, "He who shows mercy to the cruel will in the end be cruel to the merciful."[14]

As the Rebbe said in 1969:[15]

The Bible[16] recounts the War of the Seven Nations that took place in the days of Ahab. The king of Aram went to war against Israel and was decisively defeated. He thought his kingdom would never recover from this defeat. But then Ahab chased after him and told him, "You are my brother!" He asked him to come sit with him at the same table.

The king of Aram's advisors convinced him that the Jews indeed wanted to be at peace with him. The Jews, they told him, are merciful and charitable people, so they will in any case make peace.

The king of Aram thought this could not happen, since he hated Ahab passionately, and "as water reflects the face, so is a man's heart reflected in another man's."[17] Nonetheless, his advisors argued so successfully that he became convinced, and said, "Maybe it's possible—let's try!"

So, he sent emissaries to Ahab, and it worked!

And from this came later all the troubles.

This is the lesson of the Bible (for the Bible, we know, is not just a book of stories)—from the simple text of the Bible, even before we venture into the commentaries. If something like this happens again, the people it happens to can know that it already happened once! Back then, the prophet told them what to do, they didn't listen to him, and the rest is history!

The Rebbe continued:

A similar thing happened two years ago (in the Six-Day War). The Israelis defeated the Arabs decisively and the Arabs fled. Despite this, the Israelis chased after the Arabs and begged them: "Please, let's sit around the table together!" The Israelis asked a gentile to convey this message to the Arabs.

For two years already they are egging on this non-Jew, but he refuses. "Leave me alone!" he says. "I have enough of my own troubles; 'I want neither your sting nor your honey!'"[18] Still, the Jew keeps negotiating with him and promising he'll give up everything, as long as the non-Jew will agree to sit down with him at the table together!

Since Jews "pursue peace" and behave ethically, they keep chasing the Arabs, telling them, "You are our brothers! Come sit down with us at the table together!"—exactly as it happened with Ahab. Exactly the same story!

And in exchange for this (that they'll agree to sit at the same table together), they want to give them certain cities, certain territories, and certain things. All they have to do is say what they want.

And here we see an amazing thing. "And GOD hardened Pharaoh's heart."[19] For two straight years, they have been begging the gentile to sit down with them at the same table, and he refuses! He's willing to lose half his country rather than sit down with a Jew!

There is no rational explanation for this. After all, what does this non-Jew have to lose? Whatever happens, he'll sit with them, argue a little, and then they'll give him whatever he wants!

We must say that the only possible explanation is that "GOD hardened Pharaoh's heart!"

Because of all the above, we have now reached the point that they are firing at us every day and Jewish lives are being lost (may God avenge their blood). Now, we have no choice but to attack them....[20]

In summary, actual rectification can only begin when clarity with respect to these three concepts—the authority of the Torah (*chochmah*), the imperative of wholeness with regard to the Torah, the people, and the land (*binah*), and the essential differentiation between Jew and non-Jew (*da'at*)—has wended its way into the mindset of the Jewish world. When enough Jews have set their minds straight, the time will have come to join as a team to begin to change reality for the better. In particular, it is the power of *da'at* unique to the Jewish soul—the differentiation between Jew and non-Jew—that brings with it the focused clarity of mind required to begin the process of actual rectification to be described.

PART FOUR

The Heart of Rectification

לְךָ ה׳ הַגְדֻלָה וְהַגְבוּרָה וְהַתִּפְאֶרֶת וְהַנֵּצַח וְהַהוֹד
כִּי כֹל בַּשָּׁמַיִם וּבָאָרֶץ

*Unto You, O GOD, is the greatness, and the might,
and the beauty, and the victory, and the splendor,
for [Your] 'all' is in heaven and earth.*

—1 Chronicles 29:11

CHAPTER EIGHT

Chesed: Settling the Land

DECLARING SOVEREIGNTY OVER THE LAND

In Kabbalah, the first stage of actual rectification, the first day of creation, corresponds to the first of the emotive attributes of the soul—*chesed* ("loving-kindness"). The emotive characteristics of the soul relate to individuals outside ourselves. The first and most essential emotion that God emanated from His infinite light in order to begin the creative process, the first and primary emotion that He intended to find expression in our hearts, is love for others. Love for others is indeed the basis of all constructive action in the world outside.

A pure, rectified heart loves everything that God creates,[1] for He creates everything with love, and to truly love the Creator is to love all that He loves. In particular, dearest to Him of all His creations is His chosen people, Israel.[2] And so, in particular, to love God is to love Israel. Thus, the actual stages of the rectification process begin with the act that most reflects the love of the Jewish people, innate in the heart of every Jew.

The love of the Jewish people entails, as well, the love of the Torah and the love of the Land of Israel. The Torah is "our life and the length of our days."[3] Together with the

75

study and the observance of the Torah, the longing of our people to return to the Promised Land and build there our communal life as a "kingdom of priests"[4] and "a light unto the nations"[5] is what has kept us alive over thousands of years of exile. It is no wonder that the Land of Israel is also called "the land of the living."[6]

(Regarding our being a "kingdom of priests": A "kingdom of priests" implies theocracy.[7] Only when democracy does not contradict authentic Jewish theocracy can it be considered valid. The Rebbe explains that just as in a democratic state, physical life is protected—one is not even permitted to take one's own life—so too, in a Jewish theocratic state, the law of the Torah is compulsory, for it protects the spiritual life of the individual and the community. Jewish theocracy—"a kingdom of priests" (in the Torah, a priest is "a man of lovingkindness")—is based on the love of life, both the spiritual life of the people and its physical life in its land.

True, individuals only partially familiar with the Jewish religion may dread the imposition of Torah-law on society at large, envisioning extreme Biblical punishments for what they perceive to be innocuous or victimless crimes, as well as the abuse of theocratic power that characterized the Dark Ages. Historically, humanism and the separation of Church and State were a reaction to this type of pseudo-theocracy. Democracy and the Bill of Rights were a reaction to the Divine Right of Kings and the abuses of absolute monarchy. A Divinely empowered world emperor is an anathema to the secular worldview.

But, as we shall see,[8] instituting a theocracy is predicated on making the values of Judaism dear to all Jews and dispelling the myths that make them fear the Torah's vision of government. The whole Torah is a "Torah of lovingkindness"[9]: all its ways are "ways of pleasantness" and all its paths are "paths of peace."[10])

To love another soul is to love, of course, its source of life and nest of life. And so, the love of the Jewish people entails the love of the Torah and the love of the Land of Israel.

(In Kabbalah, we are taught that in the collective being of Israel—which includes the Torah of Israel, the Nation of Israel, and the Land of Israel[11]—the Torah corresponds to the mind, the nation to the heart, and the land to the kingdom of Israel, its realm of influence in the world. From this, we may understand that with regard to the establishment of a Torah-true Jewish state in the Land of Israel, the practical expression of the love of the people and the love of the land must be guided by the Torah, just as our intellect must guide the emotions of our heart and of course, our actions.)

Whoever truly loves the Jewish people and the Land of Israel, the Jewish homeland, seeks to pair these two loves—to join the nation to its land. In the Israel of today, national rectification must begin with a declaration of love for the people and the land and an affirmation of the unequivocal bond of love between them. This implies that the taking of possession of any part of the Land of Israel by a foreigner is a betrayal of one's beloved.[12]

Thus, our first act of rectification must be to declare Jewish sovereignty over the entire Land of Israel, over all the territories of our promised homeland that are presently, by Divine Providence, in our hands.[13]

It is said that "words that come from the heart penetrate the heart"[14] and that "words of truth are recognized as such."[15] Therefore, when the declaration of our rights to our land is loving and true, it will be accepted with understanding and agreement even by the more enlightened nations of the world.

THE GIFT OF THE LAND

Practically speaking, love of the people and the land and the marriage between them translate into settling the whole land with Jews. Granting every Jew a share in the Land of Israel expresses the deepest love of the people. No gift to a people is greater than giving the people its land, its place to prosper.

In order for the bestowal of this gift to succeed, after we have formally declared that the land belongs exclusively to the Jewish people, we must make every effort to settle the land by as many Jews in as many places as soon as possible. (Otherwise, we are giving unnecessary time to foreign elements to arouse opposition). To do so requires, at the spiritual level, the manifestation of the inter-inclusion of the attribute of might—the second emotive attribute of the heart, to be described—within the attribute of loving-kindness. We must be fast and forceful in expressing our deepest love for our people.

Beyond just settling the land, loving the land means working the land lovingly. This means educating our people to value the ethic of self-sufficiency and the connection to the land experienced through agriculture—specifically, through "homesteading" rather than, or at least in addition to, agribusiness. The Torah envisions the Jewish people as "a nation that will dwell apart"[16] from other nations, implying that we should strive to be self-sufficient. The Torah values self-sufficiency so highly that it encourages frugal self-sufficiency over an opulence that requires us to be dependent on others, as it is written, "The righteous eats [only enough] to satiate his soul,"[17] and "A little is better for the righteous than the opulence of the many wicked."[18]

The sages teach us: "Who is wealthy? He who rejoices in his portion."[19] The experience of wealth that comes with rejoicing with our portion renders us worthy, in God's eyes, of being blessed with tangible, material wealth. Someone who becomes wealthy in this way will be happy to share his wealth with others, as our sages say: "He who says 'what is mine is yours' and 'what is yours is yours' acts out of loving-kindness."[20]

Self-sufficiency strengthens our connection to the land, as the sages say, "A person values one measure of [the produce of] his own efforts more than nine times that of someone else's."[21] The more we produce the means of our own sustenance, the more we cherish its source, the land.

"Working the land lovingly" means working it with full regard for its ecological health and sustainability. One of the reasons given for the observance of the sabbatical year is so that the land may lie fallow and the soil replenish its nutrients.

To be sure, we can care for the ecological health of the land because we fear the consequences of environmental mismanagement. But ideally, our concern for the health of the ecosystem should be motivated by love of the land.

For all these reasons, our sages referred to the first of the six Orders of the Mishnah, the Order that deals with the Torah's agricultural laws and corresponds, in Kabbalah, to *chesed*, as "the Order of Faith."[22] (The fact that today, the Arabs, as a whole, are more involved with husbanding the Land of Israel than we are lends strength to their claim to the land.)

Regarding the love of the land, every Jewish habitation is a point of union, expressing the deepest love of the people to the land, a love of groom to bride. (In our relationship to God, we are the bride and God is our groom,[23] but in relationship to the land, we are the groom and the land is our bride.[24]) Our first aim is thus to populate the country with numerous, contiguous points of settlement,[25] in keeping with the esoteric meaning of the verse in the Song of Songs: "His interior is inlaid with the love of the daughters of Jerusalem."[26] "His interior" alludes to the interior of the entire Land of Israel, and every Jewish settlement in Israel is metaphorically referred to as "a daughter of Jerusalem."[27] Each settlement is a point of love, a point of union between the people and the land.[28]

(Just as marital relations must be conducted in privacy, so did the Rebbe advise the Israeli government, in the years following the Six-Day War, to settle all of the redeemed territories as soon as possible and as quietly as possible.[29])

JEWISH LABOR

Love of the Jewish people also means encouraging Jewish labor, heightening the consciousness of the Jewish people with regard to the value of physical labor, especially in the Land of Israel.[30] In addition to the *mitzvah* of providing for oneself and one's family so as not to be dependent on others, it is a *mitzvah* to work and build the Land of Israel. As noted above, the ideal relationship of the people to the land is one of marriage—all forms of building the land are, mystically, an act of marital union, of sowing seeds in the fertile soil of Israel for the sake of bearing fruit. Indeed, the physical sowing of the land bears not only physical fruit but also spiritual fruit (that is, new, deeper insights into the Torah[31] and good, loving deeds).

Jewish labor is the key to the solution of the greatest problem that faces the Israeli economy today—unemployment. Today, many young Jews feel ashamed to earn an honest living from physical labor. They prefer receiving state assistance for the unemployed and allowing Arabs or other foreigners to do this type of work. This most mistaken attitude must be corrected. The Torah teaches us to take pride in physical labor, especially in the Land of Israel. In the words of the sages: "One who enjoys [earns an honest living from] the work of his hands is greater than one who fears heaven."[32]

Hassidism gives the reason: in order to venture forth into the world and earn an honest living from the work of our hands, we must consciously love God, for this love gives us the confidence that He will always be with us, both giving us the strength to achieve and crowning our efforts with success. One who loves God is greater than one who (only) fears Him.

Jewish labor manifests our love of the land and keeps foreigners from our home, lest they seek to breach the profound bond of love between the nation and its land.

RIGHT BEFORE LEFT

Before turning to the next stage of our rectification process—exercising the attribute of might (*gevurah*) to eradicate terrorism—let us first note that in Kabbalah, *chesed* is positioned to the right and *gevurah* to the left. In the body, the attribute of *chesed* corresponds to the right arm, and that of *gevurah* to the left arm.[33] We are taught that the light and manifest goodness of the right (*chesed*) must always precede and encompass the relative darkness and severe judgments of the left (*gevurah*).[34] In order for this to occur, the left must enter and become contained within the context of the right.[35]

For this reason, the right is given preference over the left in many areas of Jewish law and custom. For example, it is customary to place the right side of clothing over the left side when dressing. Another example: if we arrive at a crossroad and do not know in what direction to turn, we are advised to turn to the right. Allegorically, this means that if we are confronted with a situation in which we do not know whether to respond with loving-kindness or might, we should opt for loving-kindness.

This is what happened at the crossing of the Red Sea. The sages teach that when the Children of Israel became aware of the Egyptians pursuing them at the shore of the Red Sea, they panicked and split into four groups. The first group said, "Let us surrender and return to Egypt!" The second group said, "Let us wage war against the Egyptians!" The third group said, "Let us flee into the desert!" The fourth group said, "Let us continue straight ahead into the sea!"[36]

Then Nachshon ben Aminadav, the prince of the tribe of Judah and leader of the fourth group, leaped straight into the sea, and, behold, the sea split!

What drove Nachshon to jump into the sea? Moses had told the people that the immediate objective of the Exodus was to reach Mt. Sinai and receive the Torah from the mouth of God. Mt. Sinai was straight ahead, on the other side of the sea. Nachshon reasoned: "If reaching Mt. Sinai means passing through the sea, so be it!"

The sages teach that the source of Nachshon's self-sacrifice is alluded to in his father's name. *Aminadav* means "to volunteer for my people." Nachshon's conviction and self-sacrifice came from his loving devotion to his people. The greatest expression of love is to unite the beloved with his or her goal; in Nachshon's case, this meant bringing Israel (the bride) to Mt. Sinai in order to enter into holy matrimony with God (the groom) by receiving the Torah. (In the context of the people and the land, the greatest expression of love is to marry the people to the land, as was explained above.)

Nachshon's might came from his love of Israel.[37] His might was purely a most forceful expression of his loving-kindness. (In the terminology of Kabbalah, this is referred to as *hitgabrut hachesed*, "empowered loving-kindness.")

In our context, the might necessary to eradicate terrorism must *follow* the empowered loving-kindness necessary to declare sovereignty over the land and settle it: the attribute of *gevurah* must be felt to be contained within and subordinate to the attribute of *chesed*.

POLITICAL PARTIES—PAST AND PRESENT

It is not hard to see how the four groups that argued among themselves at the Red Sea parallel the political parties of modern Israel:

• The group that advocated surrendering to the enemy and returning to Egypt parallels the extreme leftist parties of modern Israel, who see our sole salvation in capitulating to all the demands of our enemies and of the world powers. (Whether they profess to giving in to "all the demands" or just "some" or "most" of them is irrelevant, for when one begins to capitulate[38] as a matter of policy, there is no end. This is especially true with regard to the enemies we face today, who routinely demand a hand when given a finger. If we legitimize any of their claims, we indeed legitimize all of them, justifying their demand for the whole hand and not just the finger.[39])

What motivates this group to give in? In the terminology of Kabbalah, the mentality of this group is the external mind-set of the lowest of the spiritual worlds, *Asiyah* ("Action"). Here, only one thing is of ultimate importance: the standard of living. Give in, assimilate, but continue to build, make money, and enjoy life.

• The so-called extreme rightist parties of modern Israel parallel the group that advocated turning our backs to our true goal in order to face our enemies head on and wage war with them. These parties advocate fighting them physically, either unaware of the fact that there is no chance to win such a battle without first strengthening ourselves spiritually or evading this fact.[40] Promoting a military solution to the threat of our enemies, these parties do not realize that such a solution is doomed to failure unless it is predicated by asserting our rights to our land, settling it in its entirety, and promoting Jewish labor.

This mentality is the external mind-set of the next higher spiritual world, *Yetzirah* ("Formation"). The external dimension of *Yetzirah* is the seat of heated emotion, of "hot-headedness."

(A more internal dimension of *Yetzirah*—based on the awareness that the true battleground between good and evil is within us—is the emotional imperative to pit the good inclination against the evil inclination [*yetzer*, from *Yetzirah*]. But in order for our good inclination to be victorious over our evil inclination, it must first be empowered by an input of Divine light and energy.[41] God gives us this input in the merit of our first devoting ourselves to do good for our fellows.[42] In our present context, this is the loving-kindness of giving our land to our people.)

- The group that advocated avoiding or ignoring the Egyptian attack by running into the desert—to find, temporarily, a safe place to pray and meditate in solitude—parallels the majority of the religious parties in modern Israel.

These religious parties share their escapist mentality with the leftist parties, who also try to avoid the issue and crisis at hand by running into the desert of (feigned) naïve belief in a political solution.[43]

The leftists believe that our problems can be solved politically and only politically—by shaking hands, sitting around tables, and negotiating with our enemies/friends. They rationalize their position by invoking the weight of public opinion—which they themselves form.

As a rule, the religious parties are concerned primarily with providing for their own communities and supporting their own educational institutions. In this respect, these parties ironically share another point of affinity with the leftist parties, especially with their intelligentsia, who seek a more long-term solution to the problems facing us in advancing institutions of education that will share knowledge with our underprivileged enemies/friends. This, they foresee, will enrich their culture and raise their standard of living, alleviating the economic tension between us (the "haves") and them (the "have-nots"). These leftists naively think that this will cause our neighbors to respect and love us.

Because of these points of affinity, we see that the religious parties often form coalitions with the left.

The mentality that corresponds to this party is the external mind-set of the next higher spiritual world, *Beriah* ("Creation"). This is the world of ideas, the world of abstraction. Here, one prefers to run to the solitude of the desert (believing, perhaps, that the answers to all problems lie in the mind) than to cope, in reality, with the crisis at hand.

• The group that advocated proceeding straight ahead to the ultimate goal—receiving the Torah at Mt. Sinai—parallels the ideal party, the ideal "right," whose political platform we are attempting to outline here. Today, the ultimate goal is to bring redemption to the world with the coming of the Messiah. The ideal party advocates proceeding straight ahead to our ultimate goal, never losing sight of it and never being intimidated by what America or the other world powers might say.

The ideal right promotes a political platform that emphasizes loving-kindness toward our people and our true friends before any form of harshness, even toward our sworn enemies. All the steps of its platform take place "in the light of day" (i.e., Divine consciousness, the consciousness that everything is for the good, for ultimately, God is all and He is the essential, absolute good) rather than "in the darkness of night" (the consciousness only of the perilous situation encompassing us). This party, with perfect faith in God and consummate love of the Jewish people, will advance the true objectives of the Jewish people. It will first proclaim to the world that the Creator of the universe gave the entire Land of Israel to His chosen people Israel.

This mentality is that of the highest spiritual world, *Atzilut* ("Emanation"). *Atzilut* is existentially different from the lower three worlds described previously. It is a world that experiences only the oneness of God. (In Kabbalah, *Atzilut* is known as "the World of Oneness.") Here, there is no sense of independent self-consciousness—the consciousness of two—only the consciousness of the omnipresence of God.

In Kabbalah, *Asiyah* is the "lower left," *Yetzirah* is the "lower right," *Beriah* is the "higher left," and *Atzilut* is the "higher right."[44] However, since there is a qualitative difference between *Atzilut* and the lower three worlds, the lower three worlds are all considered "left" (i.e., "darkness") relative to the absolute "right" (and "light") of *Atzilut*.

This explains why when unrectified rightist parties gain power, they adopt leftist policies; in a relative sense, they are just as leftist as the avowed leftist parties.

To summarize:

Atzilut	"Let us continue ahead"	the rectified party	higher right	right
Beriah	"Let us flee"	religious parties and leftist intelligentsia	higher left	left
Yetzirah	"Let us wage war"	extreme rightist parties	lower right	
Asiyah	"Let us surrender"	extreme leftist parties	lower left	

CHAPTER NINE

Gevurah:
Israel's Mighty Hand

FEARING GOD ALONE

From the first emotion of the heart, *chesed*, emerges the second—*gevurah* ("might"). Absolute love for every Jew and for the land gives rise to the firm conviction and strength to rid the vineyard of its thorns, that is, of any threat to the Jewish people and its land, within its borders or without.[1] With the clarity of *da'at* pointing the way—giving us the recognition of the essential difference between Jew and non-Jew—it becomes clear that whenever non-Jews threaten Jewish life and the Jewish presence in the Land of Israel (even indirectly), the source of the threat must be eliminated, as Jewish law dictates.[2]

The inner experience associated in Kabbalah with *gevurah* is fear.[3] Though this statement entails a seeming paradox, the rectified emotion of fear in the soul is what motivates the attribute of *gevurah* to manifest its innate strength of character in reality. Rectified fear means to fear—stand in awe of—God alone, not to fear anything else besides God. By fearing God alone, we come to feel that God is on our side—for fear creates a concave vessel in the soul which draws into it, as a magnet, the convex forcefulness of God.

By fearing no other being, and empowered by God's presence within us, we gain the might to fight against those whom we would otherwise fear.

First, a real threat to our presence in our land, a potential fear, must spark in our souls the conscious clarification of Whom we in truth should fear. When it becomes clear in our minds and our hearts that a Jew must fear God alone, the fear of God becomes the motivating power necessary to stand up and fight against our enemies.

The less we fear God, the more we fear the non-Jew and develop in our collective psyche an inferiority complex toward him. The latent power of fear in the soul seeks an outlet, an object to fear. It is either God or others.[4]

OBJECTIVE STRENGTH

The ability to act with strength demands an objective state of strength of the people and its armed forces, referred to idiomatically by the sages as "Israel's mighty hand" (literally, "the hand of Israel is strong [in control of and ruling its enemies]").[5] In our generation, this objective state exists, if we would only not be afraid to acknowledge it! The Jewish people must firmly and unequivocally resolve to truly rule our land, not to tolerate any breach in the security of the Jewish people in its homeland. Thank God, the Israel Defense Forces is capable of eliminating any manifestation of hostility toward the Jewish people. Thus, since the matter hinges solely on our decision, any rectified national platform—motivated entirely by the love of Israel—must resolve to respond with strength to any menace or marauder in "the vineyard of the God of Hosts, the House of Israel,"[6] to eradicate any and every enemy or antagonist, for every day counts. We cannot wait any longer.

With might, we must put an end, once and for all, to terrorism and terrorists. Anyone who presents a clear and present danger to Jewish lives in Israel must be eradicated.

The Rebbe[7] compared eradicating terrorism in Israel—uprooting and doing away with all terrorists presently within its borders, whether by execution or by transfer—to a surgical operation. In surgery, the Rebbe would say, one does not cut a little bit today and then wait until tomorrow or the next day to cut a little more. One must cut open the affected area and remove the tumor at once, without delay.

No tolerance should be given to perverse ideas and would-be ethical doctrines such as that currently known as "the purity of arms," which endangers the lives of thousands of Israeli soldiers as well as the lives of civilians. As a result of this innocent-sounding doctrine—which dictates that soldiers take such care not to possibly harm innocent civilians that they must wait to shoot until they are shot at first—thousands of Jews have been murdered by terrorists hiding in civilian premises or just shooting first while the Jewish soldier stands waiting with his gun (and morale) lowered.

The Rebbe pointed out that before the Yom Kippur War, the Israeli government held urgent meetings with the heads of the military to discuss the situation. The army's intelligence pointed out unequivocally that an Egyptian attack was inevitable, and the military experts advised executing a preemptive strike that would save many lives and forestall an invasion. Despite this, the politicians, together with the biased consent of some military experts, did not accept this plan, based on the argument that such a step—or even a general conscription—before the Egyptians crossed the border would label Israel the aggressor and jeopardize its relations with the United States.

The tragic consequences of this decision verified the relevance of Jewish law[8] (as if there is any need for this). Many people's lives were lost unnecessarily, and the situation came close to being a total disaster, were it not for the mercy of the Almighty. Prime Minister Golda Meir afterwards admitted that she would be troubled her whole life because of the consequences of this tragic decision.[9]

Moreover, the concept of "vengeance" must be clarified in our own, Jewish psyche. Modern media makes every attempt to condition us to think that "vengeance" is an undesired remnant of the Dark Ages, of the barbaric past of humanity. The Talmud, however, teaches us that in its proper context, vengeance is positive.[10] When Jewish blood is spilled, God's Name (which abides in His people Israel) has been desecrated. Not only will God sanctify His desecrated Name by taking vengeance, but it is also our duty to sanctify His Name by taking vengeance. Moses' farewell song to the Jewish people concludes with the verse:

> *Exult, O nations, His people,*
> *for He shall avenge the blood of His servants,*
> *and visit vengeance upon its oppressors,*
> *and His people will atone for His land.*[11]

We have translated the last phrase of this verse in accordance with the commentary of Rabbi Avraham ibn

Ezra, who states that, in addition to God's "avenging the blood of His servants,"

> The Jewish people will take vengeance against
> the nations, and will thus atone for the Land of
> Israel, that is, for the blood that was shed on it.

In addition to sanctifying God's desecrated Name and atoning for the land, only by taking vengeance does it become clear how much we care for Jewish life, and only by taking vengeance do we raise the morale of our people and our army. [12]

In our own times, we have seen how, when the army is allowed to avenge the murder of innocent Jewish lives, the sunken morale of the public suddenly skyrockets; the army's ranks swell with volunteers and the popularity of the government soars.

A rectified Jewish platform must resolve to obliterate any immediate threat to the Jewish people. The need to assume such might, a prerequisite for national rectification, is obvious to any intelligent person, even among the nations of the world.

Before declaring sovereignty over all of the Land of Israel presently in our hands—Judea, Samaria, and the Gaza Strip—we possess no firm justification for *uprooting* all the lairs of terrorism from the land. First we must implement the attribute of loving-kindness, the first emotive power of the soul, toward our people by giving them their land. Only thereafter may we fully implement the power of might, the soul's second emotive power, toward our enemies. So long as we ourselves refer to integral parts of our promised homeland as "conquered territories," thereby giving indirect justification to the Arabs to fight for their independence in the land, how can we assume responsibility, both physically and morally, to uproot the source of terrorism from every Arab town and village in Israel? In our own minds and hearts it must first be made absolutely clear that the land is ours, and we have to tell the world so!

"AUTONOMY" PROVOKES TERRORISM

Years before the Oslo accords, the Rebbe admonished the Israeli government not to recognize or give credence to any Arab authority in Israel, not to talk with it, not even to mention the word "autonomy." He foresaw and warned that even the mention of the word "autonomy" would provoke terrorism and legitimize it. Had the government of Israel listened to the Rebbe, we would not be in the predicament we are in today. But sadly, the secular State of Israel was (and is) utterly unprepared and incapable of listening and adhering to his prophetic words.

Implied in *gevurah* is the power to break evil at its source. In our context, this means to break the very hope in the psyche of our Arab enemies that the Land of Israel belongs or will ever belong to them. It must be made clear to them (and to the nations of the earth) that "Palestine" is a fiction. By using words such as "autonomy," we build their hopes instead of destroying them.

The Israeli government must undergo a process of spiritual metamorphosis—the process of rectification we are attempting to outline here—in order to open its ears to the truth of the words of the Torah.

CHAPTER TEN

Tiferet: Jewish Law

A MAJOR SHIFT IN ORIENTATION

In Kabbalah, the *sefirot* are arranged in a structure paralleling the human body, along three vertical axes:

	left axis	middle axis	right axis
super-conscious powers		*keter* ("crown") skull	
intellectual faculties	*binah* ("understanding") left lobe of brain	*da'at* ("knowledge") rear lobe of brain	*chochmah* ("wisdom") right lobe of brain
emotional attributes	*gevurah* ("might") left arm *hod* ("thanksgiving") left leg	*tiferet* ("beauty") torso *yesod* ("foundation") procreative organ *malchut* ("kingdom") mouth	*chesed* ("loving-kindness") right arm *netzach* ("victory") right leg

In this scheme, the stages of rectification we have discussed in the two preceding chapters—loving-kindness for our own people and our land and might against our

97

enemies—are depicted as the two hands of the body. In our context, this suggests the right hand holding/settling the land, and the left hand fighting the enemies of Israel. These two stages of rectification entail the reinforcement of Israeli security, society, and economy.

All these must precede a major shift in the orientation of the Jewish people in Israel to desire to live their civilian lives in accordance with Torah values. This order of rectification is alluded to in the teaching of the sages, "The way of the land precedes the Torah."[1]

The attribute of *tiferet* ("beauty") in Kabbalah corresponds to the torso, positioned along the middle axis between the right and left arms, *chesed* and *gevurah*.

Tiferet is also associated with the Torah: *Chesed* is personified by our first forefather, Abraham, of whom it is said, "*chesed* to Abraham."[2] *Gevurah* is personified by our second forefather, Isaac, of whom it is said, "the fear of Isaac."[3] *Tiferet* is personified by our third forefather, Jacob, who "dwelt in the tents" of the Torah.[4]

We are taught in Kabbalah that kind souls derive from the *sefirah* of *chesed*; mighty or brave souls from the *sefirah* of *gevurah*; souls of Torah-scholars from the *sefirah* of *tiferet*, and so on.[5]

So, after settling the land and eradicating terror, we must turn to rectifying the relationship between the state and the Torah. This means that the state's legal system must be modified to conform with the Torah's. The life of every country is predicated primarily on its laws—"A king builds a country through law"[6]—so for Israel to be a Jewish state, its laws must be Jewish, not foreign.

TORAH LAW IS COMPASSIONATE

In the secular and non-Jewish perception, born of a superficial reading of the Written Torah that may in fact give this impression, the Torah's laws appear harsh and autocratic. In fact, however, the Torah's legal system is truly compassionate. In Kabbalah, the Torah's legal system (*mishpat*) is synonymous with the Divine attribute of compassion (*rachamim*).[7]

Non-Jewish law, which unfortunately prevails in Israel today,[8] does not know how to be compassionate. As noted above, *da'at* differentiates between Jew and non-Jew, recognizing the unique "beauty of Israel."[9] And so, in Kabbalah, *da'at* is considered the inner soul of *tiferet*. When there is no *da'at*—no identification with litigants and no appreciation of them as Jews—mercy is impossible. (Even non-Jews, when judged by Jewish law, are given the benefit of a degree of compassion unknown in non-Jewish legal systems.) The law then becomes severe and burdensome, devoid of true compassion, until it reaches the pathetic situation described in the Book of Ecclesiastes: "In the place of law there is evil, and in the place of justice there is evil."[10]

Judicial rectification must begin with the laws of monetary disputes, of plaintiff and defendant. Even not-yet Torah-observant Jews will desire to pursue a Jewish lifestyle when, going to court and witnessing Jewish law in action, they are delighted to sense that "in the place of law there *is* justice."

However, even Torah law stipulates that "We do not turn justice into compassion."[11] When compassion is divorced from the context of justice and allowed to become an end in itself, it corrupts judgment. Yet, when we sense that the essence of Jewish law is real, appropriate compassion—when judges identify with litigants and value them as Jews—we all will rejoice at the verdict, for true justice has come to light. This joy embraces both winner and loser.[12]

The justice of Jewish civil law will draw the entire nation to identify with our tradition and lend a feeling of uniqueness to life in the Land of Israel—a feeling that friends will want their disputes adjudicated in Israel, where the law is qualitatively different than it is anywhere else.

CHAPTER ELEVEN

Netzach:
Encouraging Immigration

ALIYAH IS NOT FLEEING THE PERILS OF EXILE

According to the *Zohar*, the attribute of *netzach* ("victory")—the power to overcome the obstacles in the way of reaching one's goal—corresponds to the right leg. *Netzach* is associated with the immigration of Jews to the Land of Israel, which in Hebrew is called *aliyah*, literally, "ascent."[1]

Just as immigration to Israel is called *aliyah*, so emigration from Israel is called *yeridah*, literally, "descent." In Kabbalah, *netzach* is referred to as the "apex of height,"[2] and so it is linked to the concept of elevation or ascent—*aliyah*. It is the right leg that, in Kabbalah, controls the power to ascend (walk up), while it is the left leg that controls the power to descend (walk down).

The spiritual force that motivates *aliyah* to Israel is the experience of victory over all those forces, from within and from without, that have over the generations prevented us from returning to our homeland. It is *not* an experience of fleeing from the perils and trauma of exile. Spiritually, fleeing is descent, not ascent.

MESSIANIC-INSPIRED *ALIYAH*

In Hebrew, *netzach* also means "eternity." *Aliyah* to Israel is a sense of victory over the archenemy of all humanity—death. As mentioned earlier, the Land of Israel is called "the land of the living";[3] all those who are blessed to dwell in it are blessed with a taste of eternal life. (To die in Israel is to spontaneously experience a taste of resurrection.)

Netzach also means "to conduct,"[4] as in the context of conducting an orchestra. The mass return of the Jewish people to the Promised Land must be orchestrated by a leader figure, a conductor. In Kabbalah, *netzach* is personified by Moses, the leader of the Jewish people on their way from Egypt to the Land of Israel. In order to enter Israel, the people had to first receive the Torah at Mt. Sinai. And so, according to Kabbalah, we first have to receive the Torah, the stage of *tiferet*, and only then can we proceed to *aliyah*.

In recent years, we have been fortunate to witness a mass immigration from Russia,[5] but we still await a mass influx from other countries throughout the Diaspora, especially from the affluent countries of the west.[6] A great, messianically-inspired *aliyah* is real Zionism—"returning to Zion"[7]—as this concept is defined in the Torah. Such *aliyah* depends on the rectification of the state, in particular its legal system, the stage of rectification corresponding to the inner attribute of *tiferet* in the Jewish soul, as described in the previous chapter.

Today, the Jewish heart is not really drawn to immigrating to Israel because—consciously or unconsciously—Jews do not fully identify the secular government and its institutions with the Jewish people and the Torah.[8] The beauty unique to Judaism is missing, and so the Jewish heart remains unattracted. Only when Jewish law governs the State of Israel will the country be worthy of the name "the Jewish state," and that change will immediately generate—in the super-consciousness of Jews worldwide—a strong attraction and genuine desire to ascend to the land, the paradise of the Jewish people.

ALIYAH—THE TIDING OF REDEMPTION

According to Kabbalah, *netzach* is seen as a spiritual extension of *chesed* (just as the right arm extends via the right side of the body to the right leg).[9] We described the rectification of loving-kindness as every Jew receiving his or her portion of the Land of Israel in order to truly unite the two beloved ones—the people and the Land of Israel. Certainly, this rectification also has great influence on mass immigration—not just from countries in distress but also from countries enjoying material comfort and prosperity.

Knowing that each and every Jew will earn his or her natural portion in Israel arouses the desire of Jews worldwide to come home to where they really belong. Conversely, the encouragement and initiation of immigration also serve to rectify loving-kindness. The more Jews in Israel, the more settled it can be, and the greater and stronger can be the true coupling of people and land in love and delight.

The call for mass immigration is the beginning of the tidings of redemption. Just as we saw above that according to

Kabbalah, kind souls derive from *chesed*, brave souls from *gevurah*, and the souls of Torah scholars from *tiferet*, so do the souls of the prophets (the greatest of whom was Moses) derive from *netzach*. The prophecy inherent in the collective soul of Israel is what calls the Jewish people to come home to the Promised Land.

Clearly, the *aliyah* of *all* Jews to Israel will follow the final stage of the rectification process outlined here. Only with the revelation of the Davidic Messiah and the building of the third, eternal Temple, will all Jews—including "those lost in the land of Assyria and those cast off in the land of Egypt"[10]—return to the Land of Israel. The stage we are describing here is merely a preparation for the final, consummate ingathering of the Jewish people.[11]

CHAPTER TWELVE

Hod: Expelling Hostile Elements

CONTINUING THE WORK OF *GEVURAH*

The *Zohar* refers to *netzach* and *hod* ("splendor," "aura," "acknowledgement," and "thanksgiving") as "two sides of one body"[1]—two halves of the same corpus, two sides of the same coin. Often they are referred to as partners.[2] In particular, *netzach* corresponds to the right leg (as noted) while *hod* corresponds to the left leg.

Unlike the two hands, each of which can function independently of the other, the two legs, in walking, must function together. Just as the right leg encourages mass Jewish immigration to Israel, the left leg expels undesirable elements from the land. It is the right leg that leads desirable elements up to Israel—*aliyah*, whereas it is the left leg that leads undesirable elements out of Israel—*yeridah*.

Hod, the left leg, is the spiritual extension of *gevurah*, the left hand. As described above, the rectification of *gevurah* is the aggressive eradication of any element terrorizing or otherwise threatening to cause harm to the Jewish people. But even after the elimination of actively hostile elements, the country may still have its inactive, undesirable or seditious elements—including a potentially hostile community, an enemy.

The rectification of *hod* continues the work of *gevurah* to rid the land of foreign, hostile elements. In the idiom of Kabbalah, this external act reflects an internal process that takes place within our souls, a process of purification (that is, ridding ourselves of undesirable character traits). This process brings joy to us and to the land, for the experience of joy is seen to descend down the left axis of the *sefirot* or powers of the soul from its origin in *binah* to its expression, or "reflection," in *hod*.

OUR SPIRITUAL FORCE FIELD

Hod, as said, means "acknowledgement" and "thanksgiving." In the context of the Jewish people living in its land, *hod* is our acknowledgement and thanksgiving to God for giving us our beloved homeland.

According to our sages,[3] everyone possesses a spiritual force field or aura that protects him from harm. Acknowledging and giving thanks to God enhances this aura, for the more we are aware of our dependence on God, the less our ego can deceive us regarding who poses a threat to us and who does not. "Aura" is thus aptly another meaning of *hod*.

Similarly, the attribute of *hod* is associated with the immune system of the body,[4] which, when healthy, detects foreign, bacterial invaders into the body and diseased cells and expels them.

(Even with regard to the Jewish people, the Torah says that if we do not live in our land in accordance with the precepts of the Torah, the land will vomit us out of it.[5] This we have sadly witnessed with the destructions of the first and second Temples and the subsequent bitter exiles. How much more is this the case with regard to foreign, hostile elements; these are totally "indigestible" to the land.)

Those Jews who have returned to the Land of Israel and thus experience the attribute of *netzach* will naturally experience the companion attribute of *hod*. They will thank God from the depths of their hearts for this great merit—the realization of the longing of the Jewish people throughout the ages of exile; this will enhance their clarity regarding who belongs in it and who does not.

WHO BELONGS HERE?

Non-Jews who dwell in the land and are willing to be numbered among the "righteous gentiles" of the world—those who uphold the seven commandments given to Noah and live under Jewish sovereignty—will in the future be accepted as "resident aliens" (*gerim toshavim*) of the rectified Jewish state.[6] However, those foreigners who demonstrate no such willingness—and even threaten the security and welfare of the Jewish people in its land—have no place in the country.

This phase of national rectification, though outwardly forceful in nature, depends on an intensification of loving-kindness and a positive approach (in Hassidic parlance:

"eliminating evil by accentuating goodness"). This means that as the right leg brings more Jews to Israel, its undesirable elements will *naturally* be cast out. This depends on the expression of neighborly love among the Jews living in the Land of Israel, encouraging Jewish labor, and granting every Jew in Israel his or her share.

The stronger the consciousness of the difference between Jew and non-Jew in the land—the recognition that antagonistic non-Jews, to whom the country does not belong, do not deserve *here* the same welfare and support that Jews do[7]—the more those antagonistic non-Jews will be distanced. While the Torah *commands* us to sustain "righteous gentiles" in Israel,[8] it definitely *does not* obligate us to sustain an antagonistic population that threatens our well-being in our land. Limiting the income of these undesirables will automatically repel them from remaining in the borders of the land. They will seek on their own to live and prosper elsewhere.

JOSHUA'S THREE LETTERS

The sages teach us that upon entering the Land of Israel, Joshua sent three letters to the Canaanite nations then occupying the land. The first read, "Those who wish to flee, may flee." The second read, "Those who wish to make peace, may make peace." The third read, "Those who wish to wage war, may wage war."[9]

In our days, the stage of *hod* described here comprises the first two of these three letters. The consciousness of *hod* will, as we said, lead the non-Jewish inhabitants of the land to leave (of their own accord) or to accept upon themselves the obligations of the Torah as resident aliens.

The third alternative—waging war—is seen in Kabbalah as the transition stage from *hod* to the following attribute, *yesod* ("foundation"), to be described presently. The final wars against all the enemies of Israel from within and without will be fought and won by the Messiah, in particular, the Messiah descended from Joseph, the archetypal soul of Israel corresponding to *yesod*.[10]

(When Joseph was born, his mother Rachel named him *Joseph*, which means "God will add," expressing her prayer, "May God add me another son."[11] On the physical plane, this request was answered with the birth of Rachel's second son, Benjamin, but on the spiritual plane, the "other son" alludes to the second phase in the coming of the Messiah. The first phase is the Messiah descended from Joseph; the second phase is the Davidic Messiah, whom we shall discuss presently.)

Only after defeating our enemies in full[12] will we be granted true and lasting peace. King Solomon said, "There is a time for war and a time for peace,"[13] from which we infer that "a time for war" precedes (and is therefore a prerequisite for) "a time for peace." In *Sefer Yetzirah*,[14] we find that both antithetical states of war and peace—"the opposite of peace is war"—relate to the attribute of *yesod*.

The true peace that follows the wars to be fought by the Messiah is the state of consciousness necessary for the real task of *yesod*, the unification of Torah and science, to be described in the next chapter.

CHAPTER THIRTEEN

Yesod: Uniting Torah and Science

THE BEGINNING OF OUR DREAM COMING TRUE

The inner experience of the soul's attribute of *yesod* ("foundation") is truth, not just in the intellectual sense of the word, but truth in the sense of the power to make things actualize—to make our promises and life-goals come true.[1] *Yesod* thus implies self-fulfillment and realization. The firm and stable foundation of our entire personality lies in our ability to realize our God-given talents, to fulfill ourselves in life, to make our dreams come true.[2] Our discussion began with shattered dreams. At this stage, the shattered parts begin to converge.

The goal of the rectification process we have described until this point has been to set aright the wrongs that plague the State of Israel in particular and the Jewish and non-Jewish world in general. But, as Maimonides said so eloquently, "the sages and prophets did not yearn for the messianic era in order to rule the world...but rather in order to be free to engage in the study of the Torah and its wisdom...and thereby earn the reward of life in the world to come."[3] When at last we will be safe and free, we will be able to employ our God-given talents to fulfill our life's dreams.

The innermost dream of every Jew is to make the world a home for God. This means revealing God's presence in every aspect of life, including particularly the theoretical and cultural foundations on which the structure of our lives is based. To this end, a crucial phase of ushering the world into its messianic future will be the wedding of secular wisdom with that of the Torah.

Since the Renaissance, the trend—whether manifest or undercurrent—has been for science to substitute religion. In the eyes of the educated public, the view of a distinguished scientist, even outside his field of expertise, is authoritative. If the majority of Nobel Prize winners tend, politically, to the left, this bears great weight in shaping public opinion. Before secular wisdom becomes wed to the Torah, it naturally tends to the left.

In Kabbalah, we are taught that secular wisdom, relative to the wisdom of the Torah, is feminine in nature. Before marriage, the general psychological makeup of a woman is "leftist." With marriage, the left becomes sweetened by the right. The left becomes included in the right.

Having reached this stage of the state's rectification process, we will witness a spiritual revolution in which secular wisdom in general (and the exact sciences in particular) will affirm and, from its own perspective, give full credence to the teachings of the Torah. Likewise, the Torah will shine its Divine light and wisdom into the realm of secular science, and so elevate it and sanctify it (in the terminology of the sages, "secular [pursuits] that are performed in the purity of holiness"[4] and are thereby transformed from being secular to being holy).

Above, in our discussion of *da'at*, we explained how the power of the left side of *da'at*, the separation principle, directs the first five active steps of the rectification process (from *chesed* to *hod*). Now, having reached the sixth stage (*yesod*), the right side of *da'at*—its power to enlighten mundane reality and secular wisdom—begins to direct the rectification process.

THE MIRACLE OF MARRIAGE

Just as a foundation connects a building with the ground it rests on, *yesod* is the power to connect and to unify male and female (as in marital union). Here, as the sixth active stage of our rectification process, it implies the mating, as it were, of the Divine wisdom of the Torah (symbolized in Kabbalah as "the higher [male] waters") with the human, secular wisdom of science (symbolized as "the lower [female] waters").[5]

The state must provide the impetus for this revolution by investing financially in the establishment of universities that will engage in the study of the inner dimensions of the Torah and science, seeing the two as mutually enriching worlds. This fusion depends on a "spiritual flood" of "the knowledge of GOD"—that is, on the bursting forth of the wellsprings of Torah and scientific wisdom until each succeeds in reaching the realm of the other and uniting.[6] And this will require funding, as the sages say, "if there is no flour, there will be no Torah."[7]

Here, we will experience, for the first time in our rectification process, a supernatural miracle. When God created the world, He decreed that higher (spiritual) beings and realms of reality (spiritual worlds) should not descend to lower (material) realms nor should the lower rise to the higher. With the giving of the Torah to Israel at Mt. Sinai, this decree was nullified in the sense that the Divine Presence was revealed to the whole Jewish people. This happened when "GOD descended on Mt. Sinai,"[8] and the Jewish people heard/saw the "words" of God, and when Moses ascended into the spiritual realm, the abode of the angels, in order to bring down the Torah to Israel.[9]

Now, after the Giving of the Torah, we unify the higher and lower realms in the fulfillment of every physical commandment, for God has given to us His very essence in every letter of the Torah and every one of its commandments.[10]

Nonetheless, regarding the consummate union of nature itself (and the science that describes it) with the essential Divinity embodied in the Torah, the initial decree separating the spiritual from the material remains intact. It will be so until the coming of the Messiah and the revelation of the new dimension of the Torah given at Mt. Sinai that the Messiah will bring to the world.

In relation to human endeavor in general, this means that we will be able to fulfill completely the words of Proverbs—which even now are considered by the sages to express the most all-inclusive principle of the Torah—"in all your ways know Him."[11] On the intellectual plane, this means that the wisdom of the Torah and secular wisdom will meet and unite.

The figure in the Torah that symbolizes this unity of Torah and science is Joseph, the great dream interpreter and sustainer of the Egyptian empire in its years of famine. He knew how to unite Divine wisdom with secular wisdom and succeeded in putting this union into action. And so, the messianic era associated with the union of Torah and science is referred to as the time of the Messiah descended from Joseph.

ACCEPTING THE TORAH IN FULL

The result of the wedding of the Torah and science, the union of the two realms of the Divine and the secular on the intellectual plane, will be the Jewish people's willing acceptance of Torah law in *all* realms of life. (The previous stage of *tiferet* was the adoption only of the Torah's civil laws.) With the universal acknowledgment of the truth of the Torah, all of the Jewish people will be inspired to accept its laws fully and wholeheartedly. And so, indeed, will all of the non-Jewish world acknowledge the truth of the Torah's law with respect to the obligations of righteous gentiles.

The attribute of *yesod* is the spiritual extension of the attribute of *tiferet*, as both are located on the middle axis of the *sefirot*. In fact, the connection between *tiferet* and *yesod* is stronger than that between *chesed* and *netzach* (on the right axis) or *gevurah* and *hod* (on the left axis). In the words of the *Zohar*: "the body [that is, the torso, the physical manifestation of *tiferet*] and the *brit* [that is, the procreative organ, the physical manifestation of *yesod*] are considered one."[12]

The communal acceptance of Torah law in *all* matters (those laws that are "between man and God"[13] in addition to those that are "between man and man"[13]) concludes, at the level of *yesod*, the acceptance of Torah civil law, the stage of rectification that corresponds to *tiferet*. The desire to observe the Torah stems from the power of truth—from the recognition that "Moses is true and his Torah is true."[14] This clarity must take hold within the Jewish intellect so strongly that it becomes obvious to all, and the entire world is brought to the recognition of the true faith and the rejection of its impostors. The realization of the ultimate goal will then become possible: the complete rectification and redemption of the world so that it become a kingdom for God.

PART FIVE

The Culmination
of Rectification

לתקן עולם במלכות שדי

To rectify the world in the kingdom of the Almighty

—Liturgy, *Aleinu* prayer

CHAPTER FOURTEEN

Malchut:
The Full Revelation

FROM JOSEPH TO DAVID

As we have seen, after completing the first five practical steps of national rectification (from *chesed* to *hod*), the sixth step (*yesod*) already begins the era of the Messiah—albeit the era of the Messiah descended from Joseph. That stage of rectification, involving the union of the higher and lower waters, immediately precedes the final stage of rectification, corresponding to the final attribute of the soul, the seventh of the emotive attributes of the heart—*malchut* ("kingdom").

In the imagery of Kabbalah, *malchut* reflects or "returns" all the supernal lights above it to their absolute source in God's infinite, undifferentiated light and essence. Here, the lower waters ascend so high that they reach and manifest the common origin of both the higher and lower waters,[1] the place of which Rabbi Akiva cryptically said: "When you reach the place of pure marble stone, do not say 'water, water,' for it is said, 'He who tells a lie shall not stand before My eyes.'"[2] Saying "water, water" implies that one considers them two separate waters. At this place, saying so is a lie, for here the two waters are absolutely one.[3]

119

For the Jewish people as a whole, rectified *malchut* means the arrival and full revelation of the Davidic Messiah, the King of Israel—the builder of the third, eternal Temple.

The Davidic Messiah may well have been with us from the outset of our rectification process, directing the process, but now he becomes fully revealed as the true leader the world has waited for.

This is the culmination of the rectification—the transition of the State of Israel to the Kingdom of Israel, the monarchy of the Messiah, who, by revealing Divine Providence to all peoples, brings peace and blessing to the entire world and establishes the kingdom of God on earth. All peoples will then worship the God of Israel together. In the words of the prophet Zephaniah:[4]

> *For then will I make the nations pure of speech, so that they will all call upon the Name of GOD, to serve Him together.*

FAITH IN THE ARRIVAL OF THE MESSIAH

The process of rectification we have examined may be summarized as follows:

channel of Divine energy		spiritual influence	practical application
motivation for rectification	*keter* ("crown" or "super-consciousness")	faith (*emunah*)	revealing the spark of the Messiah within
		pleasure (*ta'anug*)	experiencing a foretaste of rectified reality
		will (*ratzon*)	will to bring about redemption now
source of intellectual clarity	*chochmah* ("wisdom")	source of daring for the wise	acknowledging the exclusive authority of the Torah
	binah ("understanding")	quest for completion	recognition that every Jew is essential to building a rectified state, that every square inch of land is integral, and a blow to any part is a blow to the whole
	da'at ("knowledge")	sense of distinction	differentiating between Israel and other nations
practical platform for rectification	*chesed* ("loving-kindness")	love of the people and the land	declaring sovereignty over the territories; settling the land; encouraging Jewish labor
	gevurah ("might")	source of Israel's mighty hand	tolerating no breach of security; eradicating terrorism and threats of terrorism
	tiferet ("beauty")	source of true justice and law	rejection of foreign law and adoption of true, compassionate Jewish law
	netzach ("victory")	power to overcome obstacles	encouraging immigration
	hod ("splendor")	drive to reject undesirable elements	rejecting hostile elements from Israel; recognizing that non-Jews who do not choose to become "righteous gentiles" do not deserve the same support as Jews
	yesod ("foundation")	source of truth	uniting the truth of Torah with the truth of science
	malchut ("kingdom")	arrival of Messianic Age	full transition from State of Israel to Kingdom of Israel

Above all, we must remember the twelfth of the thirteen principles of Jewish faith[5]—the belief in the imminent arrival of the Messiah, who, God has promised, will redeem the Jewish people and the entire world. We pray for and anticipate his coming every day. Paradoxically, we are at once heartbroken that he has not yet arrived today and joyful in the thought of his imminent arrival.[6] And so we continue our sojourn on earth, doing our utmost to constantly increase merits in order to reach the critical mass necessary to bring the Messiah.

True, we wait for the Messiah in all sincerity and expect him to come today, but nonetheless, in accordance with the existential paradox of being Jewish, we continue to build, invest, and engage ourselves in long-term projects that would very likely have to stop short were the Messiah to come today.

On the one hand, the political platform presented here resembles such a long-term project. Would it only be that the Messiah arrive today and eliminate the necessity for a political platform altogether (or do it his way). On the other hand, it is our responsibility to do everything in our power to rectify the political situation and national crisis at hand.

With regard to the plan of action presented here, it is hoped that by its formulation, contemplation, and implementation, we will actually be paving the way for the imminent arrival of the Messiah.

In order for the light of the Messiah to appear, we must be vessels worthy of receiving it. With every word of Torah that we learn and take to heart, with every heartfelt prayer, and with every good deed that we perform, we become vessels worthy of redemption.

Of all good deeds, God's first commandment to humanity is the greatest: "Be fruitful and multiply."[7] We are commanded to bear children on the spiritual as well as on the physical plane. On the spiritual plane, this means devoting our lives to bringing our fellow Jews closer to God and His Torah (and teaching the non-Jewish world to become "righteous gentiles"), by radiating to all the light of the Torah. Bringing souls closer to God and His Torah includes increasing public awareness with regard to the rectified Jewish state—the state consciously preparing itself to become the kingdom of the Messiah—and building the momentum necessary to work toward it.

In Hebrew, the word for Messiah—*Mashiach*—can be understood as a permutation of the word *yismach*, meaning "he will rejoice" or of the word *yesamach*, meaning "he will make others rejoice." To live in a Messiah-orientated state of consciousness, the state of consciousness necessary to begin the rectification process, we must—no matter what—be happy and we must make others happy! Joy, together with humble thanksgiving for even the smallest successful accomplishment, is the source of the soul's power to effect changes in reality. With joy, even the hardest task becomes easy.

The Torah states that for the Jewish people to dwell securely in the Land of Israel we must serve God with joy.[8] We must rejoice in our homeland, the one place on earth where the Jewish people can fulfill its latent potential to be a light unto the nations and to bring true peace to all humanity, thus creating for God a dwelling place on earth. As the prophet Isaiah[9] promised it will be:

In the days to come, the Mount of GOD's House shall stand firm above the mountains and tower above the hills. And all the nations shall stream to it.

And the many peoples shall go and say: "Come, let us go up to the Mount of GOD, to the House of the God of Jacob—that He may instruct us in His ways, that we may walk in His paths."

For from Zion shall come forth the Torah, and the word of GOD from Jerusalem....

CHAPTER FIFTEEN

The Symbol of the Rectified Jewish State

THE *MENORAH*

The seven stages of rectification we have described correspond to the seven lamps of the *menorah* ("candelabrum") of the Temple. For this reason, the *menorah* is the ideal symbol for the rectified Jewish state (the Kingdom of Israel).

In Maimonides' drawing of the *menorah*, its branches are drawn as straight lines ascending diagonally from its middle shaft. In his commentary to the Torah, Rashi also seems to be of the opinion that the branches of the *menorah* were straight.[1] This is not as the Romans pictured the *menorah* on Titus' Arch, after the destruction of the second Temple. There it appears with curved branches, and so is the *menorah* commonly drawn.

Kabbalah teaches that curved lines represent "first nature" (which generally is not yet rectified), whereas straight lines represent "second nature," a rectified state of being. The Rebbe insisted that the *menorah* be drawn with straight branches. And so, the ideal symbol for the *rectified* Jewish state is a *menorah* with straight branches. For this reason we chose this symbol for the cover of this book.

The *menorah* stood on the south side of the Temple's sanctuary. As mentioned earlier,[2] according to the orientation of the Torah, the south side is the right side. This is a further indication that all seven stages of rectification should take place within the general context of the right. Thus, a "leftist" attitude or government has no affinity to any of the stages of rectification, whose purpose is to transform the present state of darkness into light—the light of the *menorah*—that will shine out of the Temple to illuminate the darkness of the world.[3] In contrast, the "leftist" approach seeks to illuminate what it considers the darkness of Judaism with the light of the outside world. In reality, however, this approach simply confuses light with darkness: "They say evil is good and good is evil; they put darkness for light and light for darkness, bitter for sweet and sweet for bitter."[4]

(The modern association of liberal ideology with the left side and conservative ideology with the right side originates, of course, in modern political history. However, inasmuch as everything occurs by Divine Providence, this association may be traced back to the Northern (left) and Southern (right) kingdoms of Israel and Judah. It may be traced even further back to the rationale behind the orientation of the vessels in the Temple, and still further back to its spiritual origin in the supernal *sefirot*.)

THE FIRST, FOURTH, AND SIXTH LAMPS

The *menorah* stood on the south side of the sanctuary, with its branches oriented from west to east. The west was the side of the Holy of Holies; the sages say, "The Divine Presence is in the west."[5] The east was the side from which the priests entered the sanctuary.

Holy of Holies	lamp 1	lamp 2	lamp 3	lamp 4	lamp 5	lamp 6	lamp 7	entrance of priest
west	*chesed*	*gevurah*	*tiferet*	*netzach*	*hod*	*yesod*	*malchut*	east

Of the seven lamps of the *menorah*, three stand out in particular, the first, the fourth and the sixth (from west to east):

The first lamp was the closest to the Holy of Holies. The fourth lamp was the lamp situated on the central shaft of the *menorah*. All of the wicks of the six lamps to either side of the middle lamp were placed facing it.[6] The sixth lamp was the first one that was west of another one (from the vantage point of the priest, who entered the sanctuary from the east). For this reason, *it* was called "the western lamp." Miraculously, this lamp, though being filled with exactly the same amount of oil as the other lamps, remained lit, day after day, longer than all the other lamps, and so, it gave "testimony that the Divine Presence dwells in Israel."[7]

In relation to the rectification process that we have outlined here, the first, westernmost lamp corresponds to the first stage of rectification, the stage motivated by love for the people and the land—declaring sovereignty over all of the Land of Israel presently in our hands and settling it.

The fourth, middle lamp corresponds to the stage of mass immigration (*aliyah*) of Jews to Israel. Although, on the physical plane, this depends solely on our initiative, we have explained that it can only happen after the country and its government become authentically Jewish by adopting a Jewish civil legal system.[8]

This signal of redemption to world Jewry is what is unique about the fourth lamp, the lamp of *netzach*—"victory" and "eternity"—and for this reason it is the middle lamp to which all the lamps turn, as if in anticipation.

The sixth lamp, the miraculous "western lamp," corresponds to the sixth stage of the rectification process, the union of Torah and science, the appearance of the Messiah descended from Joseph, as was explained. Here, the higher, male waters of the Torah descend and the lower, female waters of science ascend to meet and merge in matrimony. Here, for the first time, the truly supernatural becomes manifest. The sixth lamp corresponds to the *sefirah* of *yesod*, the attribute of the *tzadik* ("righteous one"), of whom it is said, "The *tzadik* is the foundation of the world."[9] In Hassidism,[10] it is explained that the *tzadik* in his work on earth manifests the supernatural in the natural world, just as do the miracles wrought by God.

THE SEVENTH LAMP

The question may be asked: what is unique about the seventh lamp (as "all sevenths are cherished"[11]), the lamp that corresponds to *malchut*, the culmination of the rectification process? The uniqueness of *malchut* is not in itself *per se*, for of *malchut* it is said, "It possesses nothing of itself."[12] This is reflected by the fact that the inner experience associated with *malchut* is lowliness, the property of King David (the archetypal soul of *malchut*).[13]

The uniqueness of *malchut* is threefold:

First, "the end is wedged in the beginning": *malchut* reflects and consummates the love of *chesed*, the love of the people and the land.

Second, *malchut* reflects all of the spiritual attributes above it; all flow into it ("all the rivers flow into the sea"[14]) and it reflects them all, and so elevates them all to a higher, Divine plane of existence.

But the ultimate uniqueness of *malchut* does not lie in itself or in its individual functions (with regard to the other *sefirot*) at all. When the priest enters the sanctuary of the Temple from the east and sees before him the *menorah*, he does not focus on the eastern lamp, the one closest to him; rather, his initial impression is that of the *menorah* as a whole. The first lamp he sees turns his attention not to itself but to the presence of the *menorah* in general. Having reached the final, seventh stage of rectification, it becomes perfectly clear that all of the stages that we have successfully passed through belong to one and the same essence. All of the lamps of the *menorah*, its central shaft and all of its branches, together with all of its forty-two ornaments, are all cast from *one* grand piece of pure gold.[15]

This is the true culmination of the entire process we have described. The seventh lamp in itself is the revelation of the Davidic Messiah as an individual. This is a prerequisite for the true culmination, the revelation that all is one (for which the Davidic Messiah comes). The true culmination is the revelation that in essence, the Land of Israel, the people of Israel, the Torah of Israel, and the God of Israel are all one. "And GOD shall be king over the whole earth [including all of humanity], on that day shall GOD be one and His Name one."[16]

Endnotes

Preface

[1] See *Malchut Yisrael*, vol. 1, pp. 281 ff.

[2] As the Rebbe states in his letter of 27 Kislev, 5741 (1980) to Mr. Pinchus M. Kalms, London.

[3] Deuteronomy 6:5.

[4] *Tana d'vei Eliayhu Rabbah* 28.

[5] See *Mishneh Torah, Deiot* 5:3.

[6] During the years 1986–1991, eight booklets bearing the title *Malchut Yisrael* were published. In these booklets, Rabbi Ginsburgh analyzed and explored many theological and practical issues surrounding the religious and political situation in modern Israel and the transition of this reality into the Torah's vision of the rectified Jewish state, i.e., the Kingdom of Israel, the objective of the platform presented herein.

One of these essays was expanded and translated into English as a full-length book, *Awakening the Spark Within: Five Dynamics of Leadership that can Change the World* (Gal Einai, 2001).

The original essays were later re-edited and published as a book titled *Malchut Yisrael* (Gal Einai, vol. 1: 1999, vol. 2: 2000, vol. 3: in preparation).

[7] The Ba'al Shem Tov is the popular name of Rabbi Israel ben Eliezer (1698-1760), the founder of the Hassidic movement. *Ba'al Shem Tov* means "Master of the Good Name [of God]."

Chapter One

[1] Psalms 122:3.

[2] The sages link the true and complete redemption primarily to Nisan, "the month of the spring" (Exodus 13:4)—"in Nisan our forefathers were redeemed from Egypt, and in Nisan we will be redeemed" (*Rosh Hashanah* 11a).

[3] *Megilah* 13b.

[4] In *Sefer Yetzirah* 3:6, all created reality is divided into the dimensions of "space, time, and man," which it refers to as "world, year, and soul."

[5] *Sha'ar HaYichud VehaEmunah*, chapter 1.

[6] 1 Kings 6:1.

[7] Exodus 15:26. In Hebrew, the initials of רפאך יהו-ה אני spell איר. Note that *Iyar* can be spelled with either one or two *yud*'s. See below, endnote 37.)

[8] *Chovot HaLevavot* 5:5; *Tanya*, ch. 12 (17a), based on Ecclesiastes 2:13.

[9] Numbers 9:1 ff.

[10] *HaYom Yom*, 14 *Iyar*.

[11] Spiritually, impurity implies concealment of Divine light and life force. When impure, one's senses become dulled. One's mind is unable to perceive truths with the same clarity and brilliance it does when pure. One's heart is closed, unable to experience true love. In Hebrew, the word for "impurity" (*tumah*) is related to the word for being "closed" or "clogged" (*timtum*).

To be far away implies that one has lost one's direction in life, that one is going in the wrong direction. In the original idiom of the Torah, to be far away is to be going on a "faraway path." One has consciously or unconsciously substituted the way of life with the way of death. Instead of walking toward God, one is walking away from Him.

[12] The second day of Iyar is the seventeenth day of counting the Omer, the day reflected by Lag BaOmer, the seventeenth day from the *end* of counting the Omer. The forty-nine days of counting the Omer are symmetrically divided by the two "centers of gravity"—the second of Iyar and the eighteenth of Iyar—into thirds: sixteen days before the second of Iyar; the second of Iyar; fifteen days between the second of Iyar and the eighteenth of Iyar [Lag BaOmer]; Lag BaOmer; sixteen days remaining days from Lag BaOmer until the end of the counting. In Kabbalah, we are taught that the rectification process takes place in thirds (all the limbs of the *partzufim* of the World of *Tikun* are divided into three joints or segments, and in the World of *Tikun* all the *partzufim* are constructed along three axes, providing for true spiritual equilibrium).

[13] See Y. *Rosh Hashanah* 3:8; *Korban HaEidah ad loc.*; *The Mystery of Marriage*, p. 21.

[14] *Igrot Kodesh Admor HaRayatz*, vol. 1, p. 617.

[15] *Sefer HaSichot 5751*, vol. 2, p. 470 ff.

[16] See Leviticus 23:15 ff.

[17] Exodus 3:12; Rashi *ad loc.*

[18] The *Zohar* compares the seven weeks of counting the Omer to the seven days a bride or wife counts after the cessation of her menstrual period (her personal exodus from Egypt) in anticipation of her marital union with her husband.

[19] In Hebrew: התכללות.

[20] See *Tanya*, chapter 41.

[21] See *Igeret HaKodesh* 27.

[22] *Eiruvin* 13b.

[23] The *Zohar* is called "the radiance of the supernal *Ima*," the *partzuf* of *binah*.

[24] *Sefer Yetzirah* 1:5.

[25] The initials of these three sages—Shimon (*shin*), Meir (*mem*), and Akiva (*ayin*)—spell *Shema*, the first word of the verse, "Hear, O Israel, GOD is our God, GOD is one." Since the name *Shimon* is derived from the verb "to hear," Rabbi Shimon may be seen as all-inclusive relative to these three. The fact that Rabbi Akiva was the teacher of the other two may be seen to be reflected in the fact that in the Torah, the *ayin* of *Shema* is written larger than usual.

Thus, the association between this triplet of sages and the first three *sefirot* (*keter, chochmah,* and *binah*) is alluded to in reverse order in the word *Shema*, which is associated itself with *binah*. Indeed, *keter* and *chochmah* are both concentrated in *binah*.

The sum of the numerical values of these three names (*Akiva* = 183; *Meir* = 251; *Shimon* = 466) is 900. The fact that this number is a perfect square (30^2) indicates that these three are integrally related. 30 is the numerical value of the letter *lamed*, and so, 30^2 may be considered to allude to two facing *lamed*s, the graphic representation of the Jewish heart (as taught by the medieval Kabbalist, Rabbi Avraham Abulafia), which we strive to rectify during the Omer period.

The culmination of the Omer period, Shavuot, is associated with another triplet of Jewish leaders: Moses (who transmitted the Torah on this day to the Jewish people), King David (who passed away on Shavuot) and the Ba'al Shem Tov (who also passed away on Shavuot). The sum of the numerical values of the names of these three personages (*Moshe* = 345; *David* = 14; *Yisrael* = 541) is also 900 or 30^2.

[26] *Yevamot* 62b.

[27] *Sifra, Kedoshim* 4.

[28] *Yoma* 9b.

[29] See, *inter alia, Torat Menachem,* vol. 4 (5712, vol. 1), p. 136.

Additional evidence of Rabbi Akiva's messianic nature may be seen in the fact that the phrase, "and [the steps of] Your *heels* [*akavot,* pl. of *akeiv,* the root of the name *Akiva*] are not known" (Psalms 77:20) alludes to the Messiah, as it is said, "the footsteps [lit., '*heels*'] of Your Messiah" (*ibid.* 89:52). The time immediately before the revelation of the Messiah is called "the heels [i.e., footsteps] of the Messiah" (*ikveta d'Mashicha*). In Kabbalah, we are taught that the uncertainty regarding the revelation of the Messiah—"Your heels are not known"—reflects the innermost dimension of *keter,* known as "the unknowing and unknowable head" (*reisha d'lo yada v'lo ityada*).

In his own life, Rabbi Akiva personified the volatility of the initial state of *keter* (in the World of *Tohu*) by yearning for martyrdom (*Yoma* 19b). Of course, he evinced the stability of the World of *Tikun* enough to know that he could not initiate his own martyrdom; this can been seen also in the episode of the four who entered the *Pardes* (*Chagigah* 14b), where he was the only one who left in peace because he was the only one who entered in peace (as explained in *The Mystery of Marriage,* pp. 240 ff).

[30] *Zohar* 3:124b.

[31] And also because on the last day of his life, Rabbi Shimon revealed the deepest, most profound teachings recorded in the *Zohar* (the *Idra Zuta*). These teachings involve the process of rectification referred to above.

[32] *Zohar* 3:291a.

[33] I.e., the Divine Presence (*Shechinah*), synonymous with the "Congregation of Israel," the collective soul-root of the Jewish people.

[34] *Y. Kilaim* 43a. In this sense, he was perhaps the most messianic of these three sages.

Further evidence of the volatility of *Tohu* (as stated above with regard to Rabbi Akiva) may be seen in the fact that Rabbi Akiva considered Bar Kochba—who was by no means a sage nor had an affinity with the sages—the Messiah. In contrast, Rabbi Meir's assertion that he himself—a sage—was the Messiah and Rabbi Shimon's dissemination of the inner dimension of the Torah in order to bring the Messiah may be seen as successively more settled approaches toward messianic activisim.

[35] Based on the episode in *Avodah Zarah* 18b.

[36] *Ibid.*

[37] Rabbi Akiva, Rabbi Meir, and Rabbi Shimon were not only the outstanding messianic figures of their generations but of the whole period of the sages of the *Mishnah.* The only other rabbinic figure of that era that also evinced messianic qualities was Rabbi Yehudah the Prince, the redactor of the *Mishnah.* As Rav, his disciple and successor, said, "If the Messiah is among the living, he is our holy Rabbi [Yehudah the Prince]" (*Sanhedrin* 98b). Rabbi Yehudah was of royal lineage, a descendant of King David, and also conducted his affairs as a royal leader (*Avodah Zarah* 11a)—even though Rabbi Yehudah himself never indulged in any material enjoyment for its own sake his whole life (*Shabbat* 118b). In all these senses, he personified the *sefirah* of *malchut.*

Relative to each other, the first three personified the "lights of *Tohu*" and Rabbi Yehudah the "vessels of *Tikun.*" The numerical value of *Yehudah* is 30, which as we saw, is the square root of the sum of the numerical values of the names of the other three sages (900). Whenever a square and its square root are summed, the result is a "diamond" number, a number that can be graphically represented in diamond form (two inverted triangles, i.e., the sum of all numbers from 1 to a given number and then from that number back to 1). Here, 930 is the diamond form of 30.

In Kabbalah, the month of Iyar is associated with another four personalities, the three patriarchs and the matriarch Rachel (who in a sense was the sum and concentrated essence of all four matriarchs). As our sages tell us, the patriarchs (and matriarchs) served as God's "chariot," His vehicle for accomplishing His purposes on earth (*Bereishit Rabbah* 47:6). In particular, the three patriarchs are the three initial "legs" while Rachel is the fourth (*malchut*). The initials of these four names (*Avraham*, *alef*; *Yitzchak*, *yud*; *Yaakov*, *yud*; and *Rachel*, *reish*) spell the full form of the name *Iyar*. We thus see that the month of Iyar is intrinsically related to the four-wheeled "chariot" (*merkavah*) of God. The sum of the numerical values of these four names (*Avraham* = 248, *Yitzchak* = 208, *Yaakov* = 182, *Rachel* = 238) is 876. When this number is added to the numerical value of the four sages, 930, the diamond of 30, the sum, 1806, is also a diamond number, the diamond of 42. Thus, the "chariot" of the patriarchs together with the "chariot" of the sages is isometric to the diamond form of the sages by itself.

[38] The story is told that once, when Rabbi Avraham the "Angel" (the son of the Maggid of Mezritch) was studying together with Rabbi Shneur Zalman of Liadi (who would later become the first Chabad Rebbe) during the period of counting the Omer, Rabbi Avraham sent Rabbi Shneur Zalman to immerse in the *mikveh* with certain Kabbalistic intentions related to the coming of the Messiah. (Rabbi Avraham was too ill to immerse himself.) Rabbi Avraham said to Rabbi Shneur Zalman that he had been told that the period of counting the Omer is especially propitious for hastening the coming of the Messiah.

Chapter Two

[1] In Kabbalah, we are taught that the inspiration and wisdom necessary to solve the great problems that face the Jewish people and humanity in every generation derive from the soul-root of Joseph, the righteous one (*Yosef HaTzadik*). By Divine wisdom, Joseph interpreted Pharaoh's dreams and outlined a program to solve the national, social, and economic crises then facing the Egyptian empire and successfully implemented it.

In every generation there is a Joseph, "the righteous one of the generation, upon whom the world stands" (Proverbs 10:25). As stated in the preface, the inspiration in writing this book has come from the clear and outspoken teachings of the Rebbe, the leader of our generation who saw reality as it is, who recognized the root of the problems facing the Jewish people and the world and advised us in every instance how to deal with the problem.

Had we heeded the Rebbe's advice, we would not be in the bleak situation we are in today. But, nonetheless, the spirit with which he imbued us continues to inspire us, giving us the optimism and the initiative to do, as the Rebbe said, all in our power to bring the Messiah. In this spirit, we have constructed here a workable plan of action, which we hope, with God's help, will be practically implemented.

[2] The very dream of living in peace and harmony in the Land of Israel with our Arab neighbors, not envisioned in the context of the coming of the Messiah, is in itself an illusion. The Rebbe, saying that we must at all times be on guard and act forcefully against the threats of our Arab neighbors, quoted the words of Maimonides (*Mishneh Torah, Melachim* 12:1), that only in the time of the Messiah will "the wolf dwell with the lamb" (Isaiah 11:6). "I do not foresee 'an extended period of absolutely normal relations with all our Arab neighbors'—other than in messianic times, when the

wolf and the lamb will live in peace together" (Letter of 13 Shevat 5741 [1981], to Mr. Pinchus M. Kalms, London).

[3] As noted earlier, the initial, unrectified state of reality is known in Kabbalah as "the World of Chaos" (*Olam HaTohu*). The second, rectified state of reality is known as "the World of Rectification" (*Olam HaTikun*). The first, chaotic state of reality, unstable in essence, breaks. The second state, built on and from the ruins of the first, is stable and lives (forever).

The existential experience of the World of *Tohu* is that of being created *ex nihilo* (as alluded to by the fact that the numerical value of *tohu*, 411, equals that of "something from nothing," *yesh mei-ayin*). As a youth, the World of *Tohu* experiences itself fresh and new. The World of *Tikun*, on the other hand, experiences itself as rectified "second nature," as a sinner who has repented and returned to God (a *ba'al teshuvah*), of whom it is said, "In the place that a *ba'al teshuvah* stands a *tzadik* [a righteous one who has never sinned] cannot stand" (*Berachot* 34b). The second nature of a *ba'al teshuvah* is constructed from the broken pieces of his or her first nature. Taking full responsibility for the breaking of its own vessels, the repentant soul continues to experience the impression that the breakage made on his psyche—"a broken heart" (Psalms 51:19). A broken heart is indeed a most positive phenomenon. It is what distinguishes a *ba'al teshuvah* from a *tzadik*, and of it Hassidic wisdom asserts, "there is no vessel more whole than a broken heart" (see *Kuntres HaTefilah*, chapter 12). A broken heart does not exclude one from being simultaneously joyful and enthusiastic; on the contrary, the *Zohar* (3:75a) teaches that true joy depends upon a broken heart and that a joyful heart exists simultaneously with a tearful one.

While rectification in general (the second state of reality) implies "diminished lights and expanded vessels," messianic rectification is understood to be a third state of reality, where the infinite lights of *Tohu* enter the expanded vessels of *Tikun*. The vessels of *Tikun* have matured to the extent that they are capable of containing and integrating, in a perfectly stable state, the lights of *Tohu*. The dreams of *Tohu* have come true in full, and even more so than one could have dreamt (*Berachot* 55b). Joseph, the source of messianic inspiration, broken by having been sold by his own brothers into slavery and cast into prison, had to wait twenty-two years for his dreams to come true.

The experience is one of continual newness, creation *ex nihilo*, and second nature at once, nuclear energy controlled and made peaceful.

With regard to the rectification of the State of Israel, the goal is certainly a messianic one. The Rebbe said (address of 28 Nisan, 1991) that in order for us to bring the Messiah, we must become empowered by the great lights of *Tohu*. In order to project these lights into external reality, to redeem the world around us, we must filter these lights through the rectified vessels of *Tikun*, for otherwise, instead of redeeming reality, we will break it. We must forever feel ourselves young and old simultaneously. The newer the new, the older the old. The "new Torah" (*Vayikra Rabbah* 13:3) that the Messiah will reveal is none other than the inner essence of the one, eternal Torah that Moses received at Mt. Sinai.

[4] See *I am Asleep Yet My Heart is Awake*, p. 3, p. 47.

[5] This provides the resolution of the apparent contradiction between the statement of Rabbi Yosef Yitzchak Schneersohn (the sixth Chabad Rebbe) that our main task is to take small steps, not to think that we must "overturn the world" (*HaYom Yom*, 2 Adar I), and the Rebbe's insistence that we indeed "overturn the world—today!" to bring the Messiah.

[6] One of the achievements of modern science has been to reveal the underlying order—harmony and beauty—within chaos itself ("chaos theory").

[7] In his essay *Kelalei HaChinuch VeHaHadrachah* ("Principles of Education and Guidance"), Rabbi Yosef Yitzchak Schneersohn lists seven requirements for an educator to succeed in his work.

These seven can be seen to correspond to the seven attributes of the heart (from *chesed* to *malchut*, see *Sod Hashem Lireiav*, pp. 319 ff and our upcoming book in English on Kabbalah and Education). The sixth of these requirements, which is thus associated with the *sefirah* of *yesod*, is order, i.e., the sense of prioritizing objectives. Inasmuch as *yesod* is associated with the *tzadik*, we see here a clear connection between the "style" of the *tzadik* and order.

Thus we see that the Rebbe demonstrated an acute sense of timing regarding the implementation of the various stages of the redemptive process. For example, he rejected proposals to implement certain strategies on various occasions, only to propose these same strategies himself at a later junction. Whereas the theoretician can visualize and "live in" the entirety of the dream at once, the true leader must limit his public directives to address the exigencies of the moment.

In our present platform, we identify the unification of Torah and science with *yesod*, because the process of seeing the connections between sacred and secular knowledge is also a process of bringing order into chaos. In this sense, our endeavor in this work to show the correlations between political science and Torah—as in our other works, where we attempt to correlate other sciences and fields of human endeavor with Torah—is but one instance of the *yesod*-process.

[8] Similarly, in our description of the conceptual hierarchy of the arts and sciences (see *The Torah Academy*), art occupies the position of *keter*, in order to "oversee" the sciences and ensure that they exhibit a measure of flexibility, in opposition to the natural rigidity of science (especially with regard to the "exact sciences").

[9] In the terminology of Hassidism, this initial jolt is called a "dislocation of the self" (*hazazah atzmit*).

This is exactly how modern science explains the Big Bang, the asymmetric "jolt" that occurred at the beginning of creation. This may be seen to be alluded in the first word of the Torah, *bereishit*, "In the beginning," which permutes to read "with a jerk of My head" (*bat roshi*, see *Yoma* 38b), implying that the purely symmetric logic of the Godhead was "jolted," i.e., was superseded by a super-rational impetus from the essence of God's will. Primordial symmetry implies a steady state of nothingness, of zero. In order to start creation *ex nihilo*, an asymmetric jolt is required.

[10] The first six stages of the program outlined here, those pertaining to the rectification of *keter* and of the mind, are all directed toward this objective of raising Jewish consciousness in order that it reach the critical mass necessary to begin the social revolution described in the last seven stages outlined below.

[11] Genesis 1:1-5.

[12] Similar to God's desire that primordial darkness and newly created light ultimately merge to become one, is His desire, in the creation of humanity, that the non-Jewish world and the Jewish world ultimately join together to serve God in unison—"For then will I make the nations pure of speech, so that they will all call upon the Name of GOD, to serve Him together" (Zephaniah 3:9). Just as with regard to light and darkness, union is predicated on separation, so it is with regard to Jews and non-Jews: The Torah's statement—that "Truly, [Israel] is a nation that shall dwell apart [from others], not to be counted among the nations" (Numbers 23:9)—must precede the messianic era, when all peoples will serve God together.

The idiom for "together" in the above verse from Zephaniah reads, literally, "one shoulder." In Hebrew, the numerical value of "one" (*echad*) is 13. Two times "one" is 26, the value of God's essential Name, *Havayah*. The two idioms, "one day" (*yom echad* = 69) and "one shoulder" (*shechem echad* = 373), together equal 442 = 17 times 26. 17 is the value of the word for "good" (*tov*), and so, 17 times 26 translates into "good" times "GOD," as in the verse, "GOD is good [*tov Havayah*] to all and merciful to all of His creatures" (Psalms 145:9).

The *Shema*, "Hear, O Israel, GOD is our God; GOD is one" (Deuteronomy 6:4), is understood by our sages to mean that

"GOD, now known and worshiped by the Jewish people, shall in time to come be known and worshiped by all peoples" (Rashi *ad loc.*). In order to bring this day closer, we must learn to recognize that it is the responsibility of the Jew to enlighten the world with regard to the true unity of God as manifest in the one true religion, Judaism, and it is the task of the enlightened non-Jew, as well, to help prepare the foundations in the society in which he lives for us to serve God together.

When "GOD is one" (*Havayah echad* = 39) is added to "one day" and "one shoulder," the total is 481 = 13 times 37. 37 is the 13th prime number (beginning from 1).

[13] Had Adam and Eve not sinned on the day of their creation, they would have entered *Shabbat* in a state of perfect bliss, experiencing the ultimate "*one* day"—"on that day shall GOD be one and His Name one" (Zechariah 14:9).

[14] Micah 7:8.

[15] Every word and teaching of the Torah is intended to relate to each one of us, in all times and all places, with regard to our personal lives as well as with regard to our communal life. Every word of the Torah directs us how to move ahead toward the fulfillment of our goal—God's goal—to rectify the present state of reality and thereby to prepare the world for its true and complete redemption.

An untold number of prophecies were addressed to the people in Biblical times. Of these, only those prophecies that the sages who compiled and fixed the Biblical text knew—by Divine inspiration—to be relevant to all generations were included in the Bible (*Megilah* 14a).

[16] This understanding of the phrase relates especially to the beginning of the verse, "Rejoice not, my enemy, over what has befallen me, for when I fell, I arose...."

[17] In Hebrew, the phrase, "when I dwell in darkness, GOD is my light" reflects perfect symmetry: Its first three words, "when I

dwell in darkness" (*ki eishev bachoshech*) comprise 2, 3, and 4 letters, respectively; its last three words, "GOD is my light" (*Havayah or li*) comprise 4, 3, and 2 letters, respectively. (When each of these numbers is squared, their total is 58, the value of the word in Hebrew for "grace" or "symmetry," *chen*.)

Continuing to contemplate the relevance of this prophetic phrase to our times, we may see here a particular allusion to the challenge of our generation to reveal symmetry in creation. Every negative phenomenon in reality (such as living in darkness) parallels a corresponding positive phenomenon (in our case, "GOD is my light"). The very realization of the symmetry principle helps transform the experience of encompassing darkness into an experience of God's light that fills and surrounds us.

The first three words of the phrase, "when I dwell in darkness," equal 663, which equals 39 ("GOD is one," as mentioned above, endnote 12 to this chapter) times 17 ("good," *tov*). The following three words of the phrase, "GOD is my light," equal 273, which equals 39 times 7 ("all sevens are beloved"). The common factor, 39, is the numerical value of the word for "dew" (*tal*), which in the Bible appears together with "lights" in the idiom, "Your dew is a dew of lights" (Isaiah 26:19). The morning dew, which falls at night, symbolizes the power to transform the experience of darkness into one of light. As noted, 39 equals "GOD is one," the essential statement of Jewish faith, which we are commanded to declare twice daily, by night and by day, in order to permeate our consciousness with the experience of "When I dwell in darkness, GOD is my light."

The total value of the six words of the phrase is 936, which equals 6 times 156 (which itself equals 6 times 26, the value of God's essential Name, *Havayah*). Thus, 156 is the average value of the six words. 156 equals Joseph (*Yosef*), the source of our inspiration to change reality for the better, as noted above. The phrase contains eighteen letters, whose average value, 52, equals Elijah (*Eliyahu*), the bearer of the tidings of the redemption.

[18] Of these leaders, while none have personified the true Jewish leader-figure, some have been "better" and some "worse." The latter include leaders who have signed and upheld pacts with enemies that have continued to be our enemies, who have given away integral parts of the Land of Israel, and who are, at least indirectly, responsible for the loss of Jewish lives. Of them, the prophet cries, "Those who destroy you and ruin you have issued from within you" (Isaiah 49:17). (See the Rebbe's address of *Shabbat Chayei Sarah*, 1975, quoted in *Karati VeEin Oneh*, pp. 66 ff.)

[19] Deuteronomy 8:17. This verse refers to the initial, unrectified state of consciousness of the Jewish people upon entering the Land of Israel: "And you shall say in your heart, '*my* power and the strength of *my* hands have achieved this accomplishment.'" The following verse continues: "But you shall remember GOD, your God, that it is *He* that gives *you* the power to succeed...."

This remembrance is referred to as the "remembrance of the Land of Israel" (*Kedushat Levi HaShalem, Peirush Nechmad al HaZechirot* [p. 143a in the Jerusalem, 1972 edition]), for it is particularly relevant to the psychological trial of the Jewish people when entering the Land of Israel, conquering it physically from its previous inhabitants and establishing therein an independent social and economic reality. While this achievement is seemingly attributable to our own prowess, physical strength, and moral determination, we must remember that our success to achieve derives from God, our Creator.

We are not meant to negate altogether our own involvement in our accomplishments, but are always to remember "that it is *He* that gives *you* the power...." This fine balance of "He" and "you" is necessary in order to cultivate a rectified sense of self-confidence, without which we cannot initiate action to rectify the world.

The numerical value of the six Hebrew words that compose the phrase "it is He that gives you the power to succeed" (*hu hanotein lecha koach la'asot chayil*) is 1449, or 7 times 207, the numerical value of the word for "light" (*or*), which itself equals 9 times 23, the numerical value of the word for "radiance" (*ziv*). The light radiating from God to the collective Jewish soul upon entering the Land of Israel, to empower the people to conquer and build the land, thus includes 63 (7 times 9) particular states of radiance (23). In Kabbalah, 63 is the value of that Name of God that symbolizes the source of all power and strength. (The first three words, "it is He that gives you," equal 9 times 63; the remaining three words, "the power to achieve accomplishment," equal 14 times 63. When written in full—each letter spelled out in the manner of filling the letters of God's Name whose value is 63—the entire phrase equals 2961, which equals 47 times 63, or 7 times "light," *or*, plus 7 times "might," *gevurah*.) 1449 thus represents the product of God's light and His strength, with which He endows His people Israel in order to build a rectified state in the Promised Land.

[20] The Rebbe (address of *Shabbat Toldot*, 1973, quoted in *Karati VeEin Oneh*, pp. 35 ff) explains that because of the arrogant attitude of "my power and the strength of my hands," Israeli politicians together with the secular-minded media in Israel are unwilling to acknowledge the many, great miracles that God has wrought with His people in the wars of modern Israel (not to speak of the miracles wrought by God day by day, delivering us from the hands of the enemies who seek to destroy us).

[21] Isaiah 9:1. The entire verse equals 2613, or 67 times 39—"GOD is one" or "dew" (see above, endnote 17 of this chapter). 67 is the numerical value of the word for "understanding" (*binah*). Thus the product of 67 and 39 implies that by *binah*—that is, by internalizing into our consciousness the truth of "GOD is one"—we become enabled to transform darkness into great light.

The average value of "darkness" (*choshech*, 328) and "great light" (*or gadol*, 250) is 289, or the square of 17 ("good," *tov*; in the beginning of creation, God saw the light to be good). The distance from the average value to each one of the two extremes, "darkness" and "great light," is 39—"GOD is one."

[22] *Yevamot* 65b.

[23] Jeremiah 6:14.

[24] Ecclesiastes 3:8.

[25] *Shabbat* eve liturgy.

[26] *Avot* 6:11.

[27] *Shabbat* morning liturgy.

With regard to the greatness of God, the sages teach that "in the place of His greatness shall you find His humbleness" (v. *Yalkut Shimoni*, Isaiah 488). For God to reveal Himself as great in the eyes of finite, mortal human beings, requires an act of infinite humility, of His lowering the essence of His absolute, unfathomable greatness, through the process known in Kabbalah as "contraction" (*tzimtzum*), so that His greatness becomes visible to finite reality. Out of His infinite love for His created beings, He reveals to us an infinitesimal portion of His essential greatness. And so we understand that the pride of God and the arrogance of humanity are verily antithetical in nature. God's pride is His gift to us, the expression of His desire to connect and unite with mortal beings, whereas our arrogance reflects only our desire to remain aloof from those around us, selfishly thinking that we deserve that all pay us homage.

In essence, God's pride is the pride that He, the Father, takes in His children, Israel. This pride links Him to His children, and through His children—Israel, His emissaries on earth—to all of His creation.

When God gave the Torah to Israel at Mt. Sinai, the first words He spoke—the opening phrase of the Ten Commandments—were: "I am GOD, your God" (Exodus 20:2). The sages (*Shabbat* 105a) interpret the very first word, "I" (*Anochi*), to be an acronym for "I have inscribed [in the words of the Torah] and given to you My very Self" (*ana nafshi ketavit yehavit*). The numerical value of "I am GOD your God" (*Anochi Havayah Elohecha*), 173, equals the union of the two attributes of "greatness" (*gedulah*, 42) and "humbleness" (*anavah*, 131).

And so we read:

I—God's unfathomable essence, which He wishes to give us in the Torah—

...am GOD—the revelation of God's supernatural greatness (represented by His essential Name, *Havayah*) to humanity—

...your God—who has humbly lowered Himself (through contracting His infinite light, as represented by the Name *Elohim*) in order to connect and unite with you, to become *your* God.

When God gave the Torah to Israel, we witnessed and internalized the Divine paradox of how God's revealed greatness is dependent on His humbleness. This endowed us with a sublime sense of God's essential greatness, His "I."

173 is also the value of the phrase "Open my eyes," in the verse (Psalms 119:18): "Open my eyes that I may behold the wonders of Your Torah." "The wonders of Your Torah" alludes to the revelation of God's essential greatness as reflected in the paradoxical union of His two attributes of greatness and humbleness. The initial letters of the two words, "Open my eyes" (*gal einai*), *gimel* and *ayin*, are the same as those of the two words, "greatness" (*gedulah*) and "humbleness" (*anavah*). Moreover, the first word, "Open" (*gal*) is short for "greatness" (*gedulah*) and the second word, "my eyes" (*einai*) is phonetically related to "humbleness" (*anavah*). Thus, our response to God's statement "I am GOD, your God" is "Open my eyes..." to behold this eternal truth.

[28] As explained earlier, this level of consciousness corresponds to the fourth level of the soul (from below), the *chayah*. This is the source in the soul of new energy and life-force to stand up and begin to act. This level of the soul corresponds, in particular, to the

soul's faculty of *chochmah*, of which it is said (with regard to God's attribute of *chochmah*, from which derives the *chochmah* of the Divine soul), "You have made all with wisdom." In Kabbalah, "to make" means not only to create anew, but, in particular, to rectify or clarify a yet unrectified state of reality, to repair that which is broken.

The numerical value of *chayah* is 23, the value of "radiance" (*ziv*), as seen above. The radiance of new insight in the soul, the first glimpse of the light hitherto concealed in the darkness, opens the consciousness of the soul to a new influx of energy and life-force to stand up and enhance reality.

[29] As explained above, this level of consciousness corresponds to the fifth, highest level of the soul, the *yechidah*. The five letters that compose the word *yechidah* contain the three letters of the word *chayah* together with an additional two letters that spell the word for "hand," *yad*. *Yechidah* thus reads, "the hand of the *chayah*." Thus, while in essence the *yechidah*, corresponding to the super-conscious *keter*, is higher than the *chayah*, corresponding to conscious *chochmah*, the *yechidah* functions as the hand—or power of extension—of the *chayah*. Only by the power of the *yechidah* is the radiance of the *chayah* able to reach out to touch and transform external darkness into light. "Single one" means "unique one," unique in the sense that it alone is capable of projecting inner reality on outer reality, of transforming subjective experience into objective experience.

[30] Referred to as "direct light" (descending from heaven to earth).

[31] Referred to as "reflected [lit., 'returning'] light" (ascending from earth to heaven).

[32] *Likutei Sichot*, vol. 1, pp. 3 ff.

[33] For which reason, it was initially not permitted to commit the Oral Torah to writing (*Gitin* 60b), in order that it remain fully flexible to adjust itself—growing like a living organism—in

accordance with the reality of the times. Only due to the fear of its being forgotten, in the dark times of exile, was it permitted to be committed to writing. But even now it is never static, never stagnant; it continues to grow, embellishing itself and ever revealing in itself new strata of depth and innovation, new dimensions of Divine truth necessary to cope with the life-situations that arise with the times.

[34] And particularly by the one, greatest sage of the generation (see *Sukah* 45b), of whom it is said, "There is one leader to a generation and there are not two leaders to a generation" (*Sanhedrin* 8a; Rashi on Deuteronomy 31:7). The one leader of the generation is the Moses of the generation, as stated in *Tikunei Zohar* (69 [112a, 113a): "The soul [literally, the extension] of Moses is in every generation." The Moses of the generation is, as well, the potential Messiah of the generation, for if the generation is meritorious there must certainly exist a living sage that can assume the messianic role.

[35] Isaiah 60:2.

Chapter Three

[1] *Shabbat* 97a. The Jewish people inherit an innate faith in God from their patriarchs, Abraham, Isaac, and Jacob, especially from Abraham, who is called "the first of all believers" (see *Shabbat* 97a). The idiom for "the first of" in Hebrew literally reads "the head of," implying that he is not only the chronological first, but that he is actually the "head" of faith in God: just as the head oversees and controls all the limbs of the body, so does the faith of Abraham oversee and control the manifestation of faith in all of his progeny for all generations to come.

Not only did Abraham believe in one God, but he devoted his life to promulgating faith in one God to all peoples on earth. For this reason, God chose him to be the first Jew, the first of the people whose mission it is to teach true monotheism to the whole world and thereby to fulfill God's desire in creation, to make this world a dwelling place for His very being.

We can now understand why faith—Jewish faith—is the beginning of the rectification process. Jewish faith entails the drive of the Jewish soul to devote its life on earth to advance God's plan for His world, "to rectify the world in the kingdom of God" (Liturgy, *Aleinu* prayer).

[2] As taught by the Ba'al Shem Tov (*Me'or Einaim, Pinchas; Likutei Sichot*, vol. 2, p. 599, 692, etc.). In the *Tanya* (chapter 42), we are taught that every Jew possesses a spark of Moses. Here, the Ba'al Shem Tov teaches us that every Jew possesses a spark of the Messiah. Of Moses, the sages say, "He is the first redeemer and he shall be the final redeemer" (*Shemot Rabbah* 4:2). As the first redeemer, the spark of Moses present in every Jewish soul becomes manifest in the soul's faculty of knowledge (*da'at*), to contact God, to know Him, in the depth of meditative prayer. As the final redeemer, the spark of the Messiah latent in every Jewish soul becomes manifest as a drive, with total self-sacrifice, to bring

redemption to the world, to eliminate suffering and reveal God's goodly light on earth.

[3] A saying of Rabbi Nachman of Breslov.

[4] *Yoma* 76a.

[5] *Sefer Yetzirah* 2:4.

[6] Song of Songs 7:7.

[7] Just as we saw above that the first super-head of *keter*, faith, relates in particular to the first of our patriarchs, Abraham, so does the second super-head of *keter*, pleasure, relate in particular to the second of the patriarchs, Isaac. Isaac's name (*Yitzchak*) means "he shall laugh." The Torah describes Isaac's love for his wife Rebecca as the "love of delights" of the Song of Songs—"and Isaac engaged in laughter with his wife Rebecca" (Genesis 26:8).

In Kabbalah, Isaac represents the experience of Divine pleasure in the Messianic Age and the World to Come. For this reason, the sages teach us—based upon the words of Isaiah (63:16)—that in the future, we will call Isaac in particular "our father" (*Shabbat* 89b).

[8] Isaiah 28:16. The root of the word for "hasten" (*chish*) in this verse is related to the word for "remain quiet" (*chash*). Thus, though "he who believes" is not necessarily overtaken by the sense of urgency to bring about the redemption immediately (for at the root of his level of consciousness he is above time), nonetheless, he does not keep his faith to himself and remain quiet. Just like the first believer, Abraham, he articulates his faith to the world, in love for all (*Mishneh Torah, Avodat Kochavim* 1:3), consciously preparing the world for the redemption to come.

[9] Of material prosperity, it is said: "In that time, there will be no hunger, no war, no jealousy or competition, for prosperity will be in abundance and all sorts of delights will be as freely available as the dust of the earth" (*Mishneh Torah, Melachim* 12:5).

Of spiritual prosperity, it is said: "for the earth will be filled with the knowledge of God as the waters cover the seabed" (Isaiah 11:9).

[10] We saw above that our first patriarch, Abraham, relates in particular to the first super-head of *keter*, faith, and that our second patriarch, Isaac, relates to the second super-head of *keter*, pleasure. Our third patriarch, Jacob, relates to the third super-head of *keter*, will.

In Hebrew, Jacob's name (*Ya'akov*) comes from the word that means "heel" (*akeiv*), for he emerged from his mother's womb holding on to the heel of his twin, Esau. Esau represents the darkness and suffering of this world, the state of spiritual and physical exile, before the coming of the Messiah. Jacob holds on tight to Esau's heel, with an intense sense of urgency to transform him, to arouse him to desire redemption, for only when Esau himself is ready for redemption can redemption come, at the hands of Jacob (*Torah Or* 24a ff). Later in his life, in acknowledgement of his victory over Esau's archangel, Jacob was given the name Israel, which is read in Kabbalah (*Sha'ar HaPesukim, Vayeitzei*) as "I possess a head" (*li rosh*). The head referred to is the third super-head of *keter*, will, by which Jacob/Israel was victorious over his twin. As we are taught, "nothing stands in the face of will."

[11] Another, similar saying regarding will reads: "There is no more powerful force than will" (see *Zohar* 2:162b; these two sayings are quoted and contrasted in *Kuntres HaChinuch VehaHadrachah*, chapter 16). The word for "powerful" in Hebrew (*takif*) is related to the word for "surround" (*makif*). From this we learn that the power that will possesses over the conscious powers of the soul is due to the fact that it encompasses all the powers below it. (In general, the three super-conscious powers of the soul's *keter* are referred to as "encompassing" or "surrounding" light, while the ten conscious powers are referred to as "direct" or "inner" light. Will is situated immediately above the ten conscious

powers, and so it in particular is their all-powerful, controlling "king.")

"Nothing stands in the face of will" affirms that will possesses the power to break through and overcome all obstacles. "There is no more powerful force than will" affirms that will encompasses and thereby controls all the other powers of the soul.

Chapter Four

[1] Proverbs 1:8.

[2] Rashi *ad loc.*

[3] The great Hassidic master, Rabbi Levi Yitzchak of Berditchev, teaches that on *Shabbat Chazon*—"the Shabbat of Vision" which precedes the 9th of Av, the day of national mourning over the destruction of the First and Second Temples— every Jew is (consciously or unconsciously) shown a complete vision of the fully constructed Third Temple. It may be added that so, too, does the soul of every Jew receive in his or her mother's womb of *binah* a complete picture of the optimal Jewish state.

[4] In Kabbalah, we are taught that the super-conscious light and experience of *keter* reflects itself fully in the consciousness of *binah* (the mother in Kabbalah, "the crown of her husband" [Proverbs 12:4]). One of the synonyms for "crown" in Hebrew (*kelil*) means literally "completeness," for a crown is essentially whole and complete. (The super-conscious bond of the Jewish soul to God always remains complete; it is never blemished by sin.)

The manifestation of *keter* in the soul's intellectual faculty of understanding thus implies the conscious awareness, with clear, unequivocal conviction, that Judaism's eternal values—the Torah of Israel, the Nation of Israel, and the Land of Israel—be forever whole.

In particular, the essential, necessary wholeness of the Land of Israel as experienced in *binah* reflects the inherent wholeness of the will of *keter*, as seen from the fact that in Hebrew, the word for "land" (*eretz*) is related to the word for "will" (*ratzon*). In the words of the sages: "Why was it called *eretz*? For it *desired* [*ratztah*] to do the *will* of its Creator" (*Bereishit Rabbah* 5:8). The longing of the Jewish people throughout their millennia in exile to return to their homeland is the greatest, most complete expression of the willpower, the existential drive, of the collective soul of Israel.

Pleasure versus pain is the most acute experience of the Jewish people as a people. Of each individual and of the collective whole it is said, "There is no good higher than pleasure, and there is no evil lower than affliction" (*Sefer Yetzirah* 2:7). In exile, we experience pain; in redemption, we experience pleasure. In exile, our very love for God expresses itself as "love-sickness" (Song of Songs 2:5; see *Derech Chaim, Sha'ar HaTeshuvah*), whereas in redemption, our love for God expresses itself as "love of delights" (Song of Songs 7:7). Thus, the awareness that *binah* implies, that of the necessity of the wholeness of the Jewish people, reflects, in particular, the level of pleasure in the soul's super-conscious *keter*.

The essence of Jewish faith focuses on the eternal truth of the Torah that God gave His people Israel at Mt. Sinai. God gave the *whole* Torah to the *whole* people in order for them to proceed in their exodus from the physical, as well as spiritual bondage of Egypt toward the Promised Land, the *whole* Land of Israel, to fulfill there *all* the 613 commandments of the Torah and thus to realize in full their own essential wholeness.

Israel's ongoing sojourn, in its collective *keter*, is thus from faith (in the Torah) to pleasure (of the people) to will (to inherit the land), all three of which become reflected in the conscious, intellectual faculty of *binah*. *Binah* is the mother-principle in Kabbalah, which itself possesses three levels of mind, heart, and action. The wholeness of the Torah, the wholeness of the people, and the wholeness of the land, are reflected in the three levels of mind, heart, and action of *binah*, respectively.

[5] "There is no truth but the truth of the Torah" (*Y. Rosh HaShanah* 18a).

Chapter Five

[1] Proverbs 1:8.

[2] This is the fifth of the Ten Commandments (Exodus 20:12): "Honor your father and your mother...." Though we are commanded to honor both our father and mother, the honor of one's father takes precedence over the honor of one's mother, for the mother herself must honor the father (*Kidushin* 31a). In addition, the sages teach that the natural feeling of the children toward their father is one of fear or respect (from a distance), while the natural feeling of the children toward their mother is one of love and closeness. The children respect their father as the authority in the home while they relate to their mother as the source of "feeling at home."

[3] See *Tanya*, chapter 2.

[4] One learns more and more of the wisdom of the Torah "for the sake of doing"(*Avot* 4:5).

[5] "The Torah issues from wisdom" (*Zohar* 2:121a).

[6] "The words of the teacher and the words of the student— whose words does one heed?" (*Kidushin* 42b).

[7] In truth, the rectification of the State of Israel described here requires no less than a cultural revolution to transform the present social and political reality to coincide with the Torah viewpoint. While the various religious parties in the Israeli government do attempt at times to adjust certain of the laws of the state to coincide with the Torah, the most crucial issues are not touched, for indeed, they are untouchable in the State of Israel as it exists at present. A total change, optimally, a peaceful revolution, must occur in order for Israel to return to its roots, to live by its Torah.

[8] See above, endnote 34 on chapter 2.

[9] Ecclesiastes 7:19. The word for "boldness" used here is *oz*, composed of two letters, *ayin* and *zayin*. *Ayin* means "eye" and the letter *zayin* is commonly interpreted by the sages as short for *zeh*, meaning "this is." (This implies direct vision, as one pointing at an object and saying "this is…" [*Shemot Rabbah* 23:15].) Thus, we may infer that boldness comes with a sense of direct, clear vision of the truth. Our sages teach that, "There is no truth but [the truth] of the Torah" (*Eichah Rabbah*, introduction, 2). The ultimate truth is the truth of the Torah, given to us by Moses, the "eye" of the Jewish people, the only prophet who prophesied with the word *zeh*: "*This* is the thing that GOD commanded" (Numbers 30:2; Rashi *ad loc.*, quoting *Sifri, Matot* 1).

Additionally, *zayin* means a "weapon." Thus, the word *oz* implies that boldness, which comes with the eye's clear vision, creates a spiritual weapon that will shoot straight at one's target, hitting a bulls-eye.

[10] This does not mean, of course, that the truly wise man feels that he is beyond criticism. The boldness that characterizes the truly wise man is accompanied by his innate sense of selflessness. A wise man values, above all, constructive criticism. But, at the same time, he is bold enough to stand up against those that mock him in his service of God. To be bold in the face of mockery is in fact the very first instruction of the Code of Jewish Law (*Shulchan Aruch Admor HaZaken, Orach Chaim [Mahadura Tinyana]* 1:1, based on *Arba'ah Turim, Orach Chaim* 1).

Chapter Six

[1] The Rebbe refers to these three as the "three wholenesses" (*shleimuyot*). The numerical value of the word for "wholeness," *shleimut*—776—is the same as that of the phrase "the coming of the Messiah" (*biyat haMashiach*) as well as that of the word "and you shall burst forth" (*ufarazta*) in the verse "and you shall burst forth to the west and the east and the north and the south" (Genesis 28:14; see *Sod Hashem Lireiav*, p. 370).

The numerical value of the root "to burst forth" (*peretz*, the name of the son of Judah, from whom descend King David and the Messiah) is the same as that of the root "whole" (*shalem*). This equivalence implies that for each one of the "three wholenesses"—the Torah, the people, and (especially) the land—to be complete it must manifest its innate power to burst forth and expand to its full, Divinely-determined, Biblical borders. (Ultimately, these borders will be revealed to be infinite.)

[2] In particular, there are three categories of Jewish law: (1) the 613 commandments of the Written Torah, together with all of their explicit and implicit derivatives; (2) the explicit commandments and injunctions of the sages of the Oral Torah (which appear in the Talmud); and (3) customs which have developed in Diaspora communities over the generations.

We saw above that "the ethic of your father [*chochmah*]" refers to the Written Torah and that "the teaching of your mother [*binah*]" refers to the Oral Torah. We now see that the wealth of detail with regard to *all* of the divisions of the Torah relates to the intellectual faculty of *binah*.

In Kabbalah, we are taught that *binah* possesses two facets or dimensions—*binah*, the power to grasp in one's mind the seminal insight of *chochmah*, and *tevunah*, the power to fully integrate that which one has grasped into the consciousness of both mind and heart. The commandments of the Written Torah (the seminal ideas) relate, in particular, to *chochmah*; the commandments of the Oral Torah (which grasp in the collective Jewish soul the seminal ideas of *chochmah*) relate to *binah*; the customs (which integrate in full the comprehension of the Torah into the entire Jewish being) relate to *tevunah*.

All three categories of Jewish law are rooted in the super-conscious *keter* of the *sefirot*, the channels of creation, and of the collective soul of Israel. Their order in *keter* is inverted. The root of the commandments of the Written Torah is in the will of *keter* (in Kabbalah, the "[infinitely] long super-head" of *keter*); the root of the commandments of the Oral Torah is in the pleasure of *keter* (in Kabbalah, the "super-head of nothingness"); the root of the customs is in simple faith (in Kabbalah, the "unknowable super-head").

As customs stem from the highest root of all, we find in the Talmud (*Soferim* 14:18; see *Shulchan Aruch, Choshen Mishpat* 46:4) that "a custom may supersede a law."

[3] 2 Samuel 14:14. At the end of days, God will blast the great *shofar* of redemption, and all the lost souls will return: "And on that day, the great *shofar* will be sounded, and those who are lost in Assyria will come [back], as well as those cast away in Egypt, and they will prostrate themselves before GOD on the holy mountain in Jerusalem" (Isaiah 27:13). With the beginning of the rectification process, leading to the revelation of the Messiah, lost Jewish souls will begin to discover their roots and return to their faith and observance.

See below, chapter 11, endnote 10.

[4] Numbers 34:1-15.

[5] *Shulchan Aruch, Orach Chaim* 329.

[6] In the idiom of *halachah*, it is forbidden because of danger to life (*pikuach nefesh*).

[7] When deciding a law according to *halachah*, it is most important to allow for no confusion regarding the rationale for one's decision. Preferably, there should be one, essential reason for the decision. In our case, the Rebbe made it clear that the reason is *pikuach nefesh* (saving lives). Though, relative to the other two, more spiritual reasons that we will presently describe, this reason is anchored in purely pragmatic considerations, this indeed is the bottom line—the value of a Jewish life (a Divine soul vested in a physical body) is supreme.

Of the "three good reasons" for not surrendering liberated territories of Israel, the first, pragmatic reason corresponds, in the terminology of Kabbalah, to the triad of the behavioristic attributes of the soul, the *sefirot* of *netzach*, *hod*, and *yesod*; the second, emotive reason corresponds to the triad of emotive attributes of the soul, the *sefirot* of *chesed*, *gevurah*, and *tiferet*; the third, purely intellectual reason corresponds to the triad of intellectual faculties of the soul, the *sefirot* of *chochmah*, *binah*, and *da'at*. The Jewish body itself corresponds to the *sefirah* of *malchut*, the adjunct of the behavioristic triad, whose ultimate source is in *keter*, the origin of the intellectual triad. (Therefore its value overrides consideration even of the integral holiness of the Land of Israel, would they stand in contradiction; but as *keter* is indicated by the tip of the *yud* and is thus intrinsically connected to the intellect, so long as we desire to be Jews and to live in our homeland, they will never stand in contradiction.)

[8] Chanukah, 5741, to Mr. Pinchus Meir Kalms of London.

[9] See the Rebbe's address of *Erev Shavuot*, 1983, quoted in *Karati VeEin Oneh*, pp. 621 ff.

[10] A "righteous gentile" who lives in the Land of Israel is called a "resident alien" (Exodus 23:33; Deuteronomy 7:2; *Mishneh Torah, Avodat Kochavim* 10).

[11] In a letter to Chief Rabbi of England, Sir Yisroel Jakobovits, 11 Shevat 5742 (1982), the Rebbe writes, "I spoke about the interdiction against giving in [i.e., giving away land] based on the

law stated in the *Shulchan Aruch* (the laws of Shabbat) #329, without regard to the holiness of the land [i.e., solely because of *pikuach nefesh*, which applies even to a Jewish community outside of Israel]. I also spoke, on another occasion [in reference to the same issue] with regard to the holiness of the land, etc. I also spoke [in reference to the same issue] with regard to the victory, which was accompanied by revealed miracles."

[12] See the Rebbe's addresses of *Motzaei Lag BaOmer*, 1980, and the tenth of Tevet, 1983, quoted in *Karati VeEin Oneh*, pp. 455 ff and pp. 608 ff.

[13] See the Rebbe's address of *Shabbat Matot-Masei*, 1989, quoted in *Karati VeEin Oneh*, pp. 669 ff.

[14] In the "reduced value" numbering system, *shalem* equals 10. 10 is the "whole" number of the Divine, supernal lights of creation (the ten *sefirot*), which correspond to the ten powers of the soul. The three letters of *shalem*—*shin*, *lamed*, and *mem*—equal 3, 3, and 4, respectively. This is exactly the way the ten *sefirot* divide into three groups of "head," "body," and "legs." The first group of three *sefirot* (*keter*, *chochmah*, and *binah*, or, *chochmah*, *binah*, and *da'at*, when *da'at* is counted in place of *keter*) is the "head"; the second group of three *sefirot* (*chesed*, *gevurah*, and *tiferet*) is the "body"; the third group of four *sefirot* (*netzach*, *hod*, *yesod*, and *malchut*) is the "legs."

The reduced value of the word *shalom*, possessing an additional *vav*, is 16. In the normative numbering system, the first letter (*yud*) of God's essential Name *Havayah* equals 10; the remaining three letters (*hei*, *vav*, *hei*) equal 16. Thus the root *shalem* ("wholeness") and its most important derivative, *shalom* ("peace"), perfectly reflect the secret of the first letter of *Havayah* (*yud* = 10) and its remaining letters (*hei vav hei* = 16). And so we see that God's essential Name *Havayah* conveys the truth that peace depends on (and derives from) wholeness. The wholeness of the *yud* is reflected in the three letters *hei vav hei*, which themselves correspond to the three "wholes" of the Torah (the first *hei*), the people (the *vav*), and the land (the final *hei*).

[15] *Yevamot* 65b.

[16] As it is written, "He shall make peace for Me; peace he shall make for Me" (Isaiah 27:5; *Sanhedrin* 99b).

[17] Ironically, the leftist slogan *shalom chaver* ("peace, friend") numerically equals Jerusalem (*Yerushalaim*, 586), whose original name was "[the city of] peace" (*Shalem*). This was the name given it by Melchizedek, the king of Salem. Abraham, the first Jew, added to this name the three letters *Yeru*, from the word "to see" (*yireh*) or "to fear" (*yirah*). This is the holy site where God appeared to Abraham at the Binding of Isaac. Here, Abraham witnessed the Divine Presence and stood in awe of God. The full name, Jerusalem, thus means "perfect awe," alluding to the peace that will come to Israel and to all of mankind when, and only when, we witness God's Providence and we come to stand before Him in awe.

First, all of Israel must become true friends—"All of Israel are friends" (*chaverim kol Yisrael* [Liturgy, blessing for the new month]). The word for "friend" (*chaver*) is from the root "to connect." Of Jerusalem is said, "the city that is connected together" (*ir shechubrah lah yachdav* [Psalms 122:3]). When Jews become friends, Jerusalem (i.e., its east and west sides) shall become connected and one. One Jerusalem includes, of course, the Temple Mount (the site of the Binding of Isaac). As the sages teach, it is the Temple Mount that makes Jerusalem one and the whole Land of Israel one. With exclusive Jewish possession of the Temple Mount will come the building of the Temple itself. Only then will all peoples flow to worship the one God of Israel in Jerusalem (Isaiah 2:3) and "My house will be called a house of prayer for all nations" (*ibid.* 56:7). Then will all nations be friends and serve God together (Zephaniah 3:9).

To continue the irony, the combined numerical value of "peace, friend" (*shalom chaver*, 586) and "peace now" (*shalom achshav*, 772) is equal to that of the second verse of the *Shema*, "Blessed be the Name of the glory of His kingdom forever and ever" (1358). In Kabbalah, this verse expresses "the lower unification," i.e., the revelation of God's unity permeating all of reality by means of the glory of His kingdom, His Providence over each and every one of His creations. (1358 = 7 times 194; 194 equals *tzedek*, "righteousness," a connotation, in Kabbalah, of *malchut*, God's kingdom on earth.) In Kabbalah, the numerical equivalence of two words or phrases implies that the two are either identical or antithetical. Here, the numerical equivalence teaches us that false calls to peace (and the ideology on which they are based) preclude the revelation of God's Kingdom on earth.

[18] Jeremiah 6:14.

[19] The opening words of Rashi's commentary on the Torah are:

> The Torah should have begun from "This month shall be for you the first of the months" (Exodus 12:2), for this is the first commandment given to the Jewish people. Why, then, did it begin with the story of creation? Because "He recounted the strength of His deeds in order to give them the inheritance of the nations" (Psalms 111:6). That is, if the nations of the world say to the Jews, "You are thieves! For you have captured the lands of seven nations!" they can retort, "The whole world is God's. He created it and gave it to whom He chose. It was His desire to give it to them and it was His desire to take it from them and give it to us!"

The Rebbe explains that when we proclaim this unabashedly to everyone, this makes an impact on the collective unconscious of the nations to acknowledge the truth. The collective unconscious of the nations then influences their collective consciousness to openly acknowledge our rights to the land. (See the Rebbe's address of *Motzaei Shabbat Bereishit*, 1977, quoted in *Karati VeEin Oneh*, pp. 153 ff.)

Secondly, in the Torah's account of the spies who spied out the Land of Israel (Numbers 13), we read:

...They went up through the Negev and came to Hebron. Achiman, Sheishai, and Talmai, the children of the giants, were there....

When the spies reported what they had seen to the people, they said:

"...And there we saw the fallen ones, the giants who fell [from heaven]. We felt like grasshoppers next to them, and so did we seem to them."

On this verse, Rashi comments:

"We heard them say to each other, 'There are ants in the vineyards that look like men.'"

Rabbi Levi Yitzchak of Berditchev (*Kedushat Levi, Shelach, s.v. O Yevu'ar* [79b]) remarks on Rashi's comment:

Why does Rashi mention ants when the Torah speaks of grasshoppers? The explanation is apparently as follows. It is told in the Midrash (*Yalkut Shimoni*, Numbers 742) that Talmai said to the spies: "Why do you want to conquer the Land of Israel? After all, the whole world belongs to God and He gave this land to us. It would therefore be stolen property if you took it." Now, our sages have stated on the verse, "Go to the ant, consider her ways..." (Proverbs 6:6) that [even if, God forbid, the Torah had not been given to us,] we could derive the prohibition against theft from the ant's behavior. Ants do not take another's property (*Eiruvin* 100b). Thus, when Rashi says that the spies overheard the giants saying "there are ants in the vineyards that look like men," he means that they said that "the people we see in the vineyards eschew robbery, just as ants do. Therefore, [if we convince them that they would be robbing it from us,] they will not take the Land of Israel from us," as the Midrash reports that Talmai indeed said to them.

The truth, of course, is not so, as Rashi states in his [first] comment on Genesis: "It was His desire to give it to them and it was His desire to...give it to" Israel, and it is therefore not robbery.

Thus, we see that it is indeed easy for non-Jews to play upon the Jews' aversion to immoral behavior and dupe them into thinking they would be thieves were they to lay claim to what is in fact rightfully theirs. The only way we can overcome this exploitation of our natural inferiority complex is by boldly anchoring ourselves in the Torah's "wisdom [that] emboldens the wise" (Ecclesiastes 7:19, as quoted and explained above).

[20] See Deuteronomy 8:14.

[21] See the Rebbe's addresses of *Shabbatot Matot* and *Masei*, 1970 and 1977, quoted in *Karati VeEin Oneh*, pp. 7 ff and 137 ff.

[22] *Bava Batra* 10b.

[23] See the Rebbe's address of *Shabbat Emor*, 1974, quoted in *Karati VeEin Oneh*, pp. 37 ff.

[24] Boldness also implies the strength of character and conviction necessary to continuously be on guard and ready to fight, physically, for our right to inherit our land. In the face of the enemy we must be as "bold as a tiger" (*Avot* 5:20), making it absolutely clear to him that we are fully prepared to fight for our cause. The Rebbe explains (address of 24 Tevet, 1978, quoted in *Karati VeEin Oneh*, pp. 173 ff) that this is the only way to achieve lasting peace. The enemy raises its hands before Jewish boldness. The sages have made it clear that "there is no trust in the nations" (*Chulin* 133b), especially with regard to sworn enemies who claim rights to the Land of Israel.

[25] Psalms 29:11.

[26] See the Rebbe's address of 19 Kislev, 1975, quoted in *Karati VeEin Oneh*, pp. 73 ff.

Chapter Seven

[1] This level of knowledge is referred to in Kabbalah as the "lower knowledge" (*da'at tachton*) or as the "extended knowledge" (*da'at hamitpashet*), in contrast to the "higher knowledge" (*da'at elyon*) or the "hidden knowledge" (*da'at hane'elam*) that unites, in the mind, the two intellectual faculties of *chochmah* and *binah*.

[2] The primordial sin of Adam and Eve, the eating of the forbidden fruit of the Tree of Knowledge of Good and Evil, resulted in the confusion of the boundaries intended to separate good from evil. Good and evil mixed together. There no longer existed pure, unadulterated good, only a polluted state of good, which, due to its existential state of pollution—its "impure spirit"—is doomed to death. This fallen state of good will only be rectified in the end of days, when the impure spirit will be removed from the earth (Zechariah 13:2) and the dead will be resurrected.

We are taught in Kabbalah that the fruit of the Tree of Knowledge would have become permissible to Adam and Eve at the onset of *Shabbat*, a mere three hours after they sinned. Had they waited and eaten the fruit on *Shabbat*, the result would have been the positive union (i.e., "knowledge") of good and evil. The very root of evil would have been transformed into good and the union of the two would have given birth to holy offspring ("very good," i.e., super-good).

[3] In the Jewish people as a whole, this is the union of *tzadikim* ("righteous ones," that have never sinned and have succeeded in uprooting the evil inclination from their hearts) and *ba'alei teshuvah* (those who have sinned, but who have returned to God in truth, abandoning their evil ways forever).

The initial letters of *ba'al teshuvah* spell the word for "daughter" (*bat*). The *ba'al teshuvah* is referred to in the Bible as "the daughter

of Zion" (Zechariah 2:14, *inter alia*). The *tzadik* is "the son of
Zion" (Joel 2:23, *inter alia*) who courts and marries "the daughter
of Zion" (for "it is the way of man to search for and court woman
[his 'lost side']" [*Kidushin* 2b]). From their union are born the "new
souls" of the future, whose level of Divine consciousness will
greatly exceed that of the souls of the present.

Every individual soul possesses its own *tzadik* and *ba'al
teshuvah*. The *tzadik* in each of us is the consciousness of a pristine
state of purity (of soul and body), an undefiled sense of oneness
with God. The *ba'al teshuvah* in each of us is the consciousness of
our having fallen from our pristine state, far away from being one
with God, and having now to dedicate our lives to climb back and
come close to God. In our Divine service, the manifestation of the
ba'al teshuvah within must generally precede the revelation of the
potential *tzadik* within (for, only after the initial appearance of
woman is it "the way of man [to appear and] to search for and
court woman" [*Kidushin* 2b], as explained in *Tanya*, chapter 43).
This is alluded to in the saying of the sages that "a daughter first
[to be born] is a good sign for sons [to be born thereafter]" (*Bava
Batra* 141a). First, we must bear in our hearts the consciousness of
the *ba'al teshuvah*, "the daughter of Zion," and thereafter we will
merit the revelation in our hearts of "the sons of Zion."

Indeed, according to Kabbalah, there are six sons in the heart
and one daughter. The six sons are the six emotive attributes from
chesed to *yesod*. The daughter is *malchut*. Although in the order of the
stages of the actual process of rectification *malchut* comes last, as an
ideal goal its consciousness in the soul must be born first, for "the
end of action is first in thought" (Liturgy of *Kabbalat Shabbat*,
Lechah Dodi). With regard to the collective Jewish soul, the drive to
establish the kingdom of God on earth is the motivating power of
true *teshuvah* to God, "return from love" (*Yoma* 86a).

[4] See *Tanya*, end of chapter 43, where it is stated that in
general, it is the left side of *da'at* that manifests itself before the
right side.

[5] This is the beginning of the existential "sweetening" of all reality.

[6] *Y. Berachot* 5:2.

[7] *Havdalah* blessing.

[8] Exodus 19:6. Of the first Jew, Abraham, it is said, "you shall be a priest forever" (Psalms 110:4). To be a priest to all nations on earth, one must love all creation and desire and be able to bring God's light to humanity. These are the characteristics of Abraham, from whom we, the Jewish people, have inherited them. The blessing that the Jewish people be "a *kingdom* of priests" directly preceded the giving of the Torah to Israel at Mt. Sinai. Only by the power of the Torah do we become a ruling kingdom to bring the word of God to others.

The numerical value of "a kingdom of priests" (*mamlechet kohanim*), 655, is equal to that of the general appellation for God in rabbinic literature, "The Holy One, blessed be He" (*HaKadosh baruch Hu*). This alludes to the fact that with the giving of the Torah, the Jewish people was imbued with Divine power to serve as "a kingdom of priests" for all of humanity. A priest possesses the power to unite with God's essential holiness, His unique Oneness, and reveal it to all—this being the meaning of "to bless": to "bring down." This is how Kabbalah explains the meaning of the appellation, "The Holy One, *blessed* be He."

[9] When the Rebbe was asked to define the difference between Jew and non-Jew, he would answer that a Jew is in essence a giver while a non-Jew is in essence a receiver.

[10] This fact appears in *halachah* with regard to the law of writing a *prozbul* (see *Mishneh Torah, Shemitah veYovel* 9:15 on; *Shulchan Aruch, Choshen Mishpat* 67; the Rebbe's address of Purim, 1970, quoted in *Karati VeEin Oneh*, pp. 4 ff). From this, the Rebbe learns that every Jew, no matter where he lives, has a say regarding all issues pertaining to the Land of Israel—with the exception of giving away God-given land. No Jew may give away parts of the

Land of Israel for this is forbidden by the Torah, to which all Jews are obligated.

Moreover, all Jews are obligated to protest against wrongdoings in Israel—to cry out in pain, even when we know that our words will not be heeded, for we are partial owners of the land. We, the Jewish people, are all one living organism, and when one limb is ill, all of the limbs of the body experience the pain (see the Rebbe's address of 19 Kislev, 1970, quoted in *Karati VeEin Oneh*, pp. 22 ff).

[11] The Ba'al Shem Tov taught that just as we must believe in God even though we do not see Him, so must we believe in the spark of Godliness innate in every Jew even though this may be not at all apparent. The Ba'al Shem Tov and his successors, especially beginning with Rabbi Shneur Zalman of Liadi, revealed this faith and succeeded in transforming it into knowledge.

[12] See below (chapter 12) with regard to the attribute of *hod*, which corresponds to the immune system in the body, whose function is to distinguish between friend and foe.

[13] In the orientation of the Torah, "left" is north and "right" is south. In ancient Israel, the northern kingdom was relatively more secular and leftist compared to the more religious southern kingdom.

[14] *Midrash Tanchuma, Metzora* 1.

[15] Address of *Shabbat Matot-Masei*, 1969, quoted in *Karati VeEin Oneh*, pp. 1 ff.

[16] 1 Kings 20:32.

[17] Proverbs 27:19.

[18] *Midrash Tanchuma, Balak* 6.

[19] Exodus 9:12, 10:20-27; 11:10, 14:8.

[20] "...the way [that is, with the same forcefulness with which] the Torah describes [how the tribe of Gad, the commandos in the

original conquest of the Land of Israel, were to kill the Canaanite enemy]: 'cut off their arm together with their skull'" (Deuteronomy 33:20).

The Rebbe had recently initiated his famous *tefilin* campaign, citing Rabbeinu Asher (*Halachot Ketanot, hilchot tefilin*) who interpreted this verse to mean that putting on *tefilin* (on the arm and the head) helps the Jewish war effort (i.e., cutting off the enemy's arm and head) by invoking God's mercy to give courage and power to the Jewish forces.

The Rebbe continued:

Moreover:

They want to divide Jerusalem into three parts, that is, so that it will be a city of Christians, Muslims, and Jews.

Jerusalem belongs since time immemorial to the Jews. It began with Shem, Noah's son; Melchizedek, the king of Salem; Abraham; and then King David conquered it from the Jebusites. The non-Jews themselves have written that King David conquered Jerusalem thousands of years ago!

How is it possible to let a non-Jew into Jerusalem? Jewish law states that it is forbidden for a non-Jew to live in Jerusalem!

True, this law applies only when "the Jew has the upper hand" [Cf. *Ketubot* 26b ff; *Bava Kama* 97b, etc.], while when this is not the case we cannot remove them. But that doesn't mean that we have to *encourage* them to live there. When the non-Jew asserts that he'd rather not live in Jerusalem and wants to leave, we don't have to chase after him and beg him to stay, promising that we'll build him a house, give him funds, and rebuild the ruins of his "house of prayer" that is in ruins so long that everyone has already forgotten about it, even the non-Jews themselves.

Do you want to do the gentiles a favor? It is not good for gentiles to live in Jerusalem; it's an affront to their very being!

The Israeli government settles gentiles (God preserve us) in the precincts of the Temple, a place too holy for even a Jew to enter!

...And because of all this, the Jews can no longer rely on [God's promise that] "they will fear you" [Deuteronomy 28:10], but now have no choice but to make use of [His directive to] "cut off their arm together with their skull." In other words [that is, spiritually, for all physical rectification must be predicated by spiritual rectification], we must first rectify [in ourselves, before applying the directive to our enemies] the way *we* act—the arm, and then the way *we* think—the skull.

Chapter Eight

[1] All of creation came into being, in essence, on the first day, as stated in the very first verse of the Torah: "In the beginning God created the heavens and the earth" (Genesis 1:1). The sages teach us that "the heavens and the earth" implies "and everything therein" (see Rashi on Genesis 1:14).

[2] *HaYom Yom*, 28 Nisan.

[3] Liturgy for the Evening Service.

[4] Exodus 19:5-6.

[5] Isaiah 49:6.

[6] Psalms 116:9: "I will walk before GOD in the land of the living." "The land of the living" literally reads "the *lands* of the living" (*artzot hachaim*), in the plural, alluding to two lands: the spiritual Land of Israel above and the physical Land of Israel below (*Yahel Or* on this verse, quoting Rabbi Shneur Zalman of Liadi; see also *Igeret HaKodesh* 14). King David "walked before GOD"—that is, he was always conscious of God's Presence and Providence. By virtue of his awareness of the integral interdependence of the higher land (in Kabbalah, *binah*) and the lower land (in Kabbalah, *malchut*), the intention of his mind and will of his heart (the higher land) radiated in all of his actions (the lower land).

Numerically, "the land of the living" (*eretz hachaim*) equals 364 = 14 times 26, "the hand [*yad* = 14] of GOD [*Havayah* = 26]." "The lands of the living," *artzot hachaim*, equals 770 = 7 times 110, 7 miracles (for "miracle," *nes*, equals 110), alluding to the fact that in Israel, by virtue of the manifest union of its two dimensions of land, God's Providence over the land is miraculous. This is because each one of the seven attributes of creation, corresponding to the seven emotions of the heart, is elevated from the realm of the natural to the realm of the supernatural. "The Land of Israel" (*eretz Yisrael*) equals 832 = 32 times 26, "the heart [*lev* = 32] of GOD [*Havayah* = 26]." From the infinite goodness of God's heart, and by His outstretched hand, He gives life to the People of Israel who dwell in His land.

[7] Address of Simchat Torah, 1975, quoted in *Karati VeEin Oneh*, pp. 55 ff.

[8] Chapters 10 and 13.

[9] Proverbs 31:26.

[10] *Ibid.* 3:17.

[11] In essence, all three—the Torah of Israel, the Nation of Israel, and the Land of Israel—are different manifestations of one Divine being. A beautiful numerical phenomenon alludes to this: The word for "one" in Hebrew (*echad*) equals 13. "The Torah of Israel" (*Torat Israel*) equals 1547 = 13 times 119; "the Congregation of Israel" (*Kehal Israel*, the more common idiom for the Jewish nation in the Torah) equals 676 = 13 times 52 = 26 (the value of God's essential Name, *Havayah*) squared; "the Land of Israel" (*Eretz Israel*) equals 13 times 64. All three are multiples of 13, which, of course, is *echad* ("one")!

Neither the word for "congregation" or "land" by itself is a multiple of 13, but *Torah* equals 611 = 13 times 47. The sum of the three phrases, "the Torah of Israel," "the Congregation of Israel," and "the Land of Israel" is 3055 which equals 5 times 611, five times *Torah*, alluding to the five books of the Torah. This teaches us that all is included in the Torah, in the Divine mind of Israel, just as a child (the Jewish people) and his or her destiny on earth (the Land of Israel) are included in the mind of the father. The Torah is the essence of the consciousness of "one," and from it, Divine oneness is reflected in the people and the land, as it is said, "one nation in the land" (2 Samuel 7:23).

[12] The seventh of the Ten Commandments is "You shall not commit adultery" (*lo tinaf*). Numerically, this commandment equals

the word for "Zionism" (*Tzionut*, 562). This teaches us that true, Torah-oriented Zionism demands the firm resolution not to commit adultery on any level. With regard to the settling of the land, this means not allowing foreign elements to breach our bond of love to our land.

[13] See *Malchut Yisrael*, vol. 1, pp. 233 ff. In the Six-Day War, God returned to His chosen people the entire West Bank of the Jordan, thereby expanding the borders of Israel to approximate those areas conquered by Joshua when the people first entered the Promised Land.

These were the borders of the land then inhabited by the seven Canaanite nations, who, in Kabbalah, correspond to the seven emotive attributes of the unrectified heart. Within these borders, it is the task of the Jewish people to rectify, on the communal level, the seven emotions (which is the underlying motif of the seven-stage political platform presented here).

The full borders of the Promised Land, the borders promised by God to Abraham in the Covenant of the Pieces, are from the Nile to the Euphrates (Genesis 15:18). In addition to the above seven Canaanite nations, another three nations are included in God's promise to Abraham: the Keinites, the Kenizites, and the Kadmonites. In Kabbalah, these three nations correspond to the three levels of consciousness above the emotions of the heart.

Before the coming of the Messiah, these three faculties of the soul cannot be fully rectified on the communal level, and so the extended borders of Israel cannot yet be realized.

We have explained above that the stages of rectification on the communal level associated with the seven emotive attributes—the seven practical stages of the political platform presented here—are predicated on the reorientation of the Jewish super-conscious (*keter*) and conscious mind to desire true and complete redemption and to understand the intellectual principles upon which it is based. This process occurs primarily on the individual plane. When enough Jews come to know (at the level of their soul's super-conscious and conscious mind) Judaism's true objective and value-system, then, the practical, seven-stage process can begin.

This, however, is not yet the complete rectification of the three powers of *keter* and the mind. (*Keter* includes all three facets of faith, pleasure, and will; *chochmah* and *binah* include *da'at*, the power that unites them and links them to the emotions of the heart.) In Kabbalah, we are taught that the complete rectification of the higher three powers of the soul occurs when they become manifest as essentially transcendent with respect to the practical side of the soul. They are no longer meant to be "applied," that is, attuned to direct the heart to the rectification of its seven emotive attributes. This has already been accomplished. Now, they are solely attuned to perceive the infinite light of God's transcendent essence as it is reflected in reality.

At the point described, we are ready to inherit the full borders of Israel, the entire land once inhabited by the ten nations promised to Abraham, from the Nile to the Euphrates. This stage follows and continues the last of the seven practical stages of rectification described here, the State of Israel having been fully transformed to become the Kingdom of Israel—the Kingdom of God on earth.

After reaching the borders promised to Abraham, we are taught (see *Pesikta Rabati, Shabbat veRosh Chodesh* 3) that, ultimately, the borders of Israel will expand to encompass the whole earth. Our consciousness will rise to perceive God's infinite light above even the level of *keter*. This is when all nations will "speak one tongue and serve GOD together" (Zephaniah 3:12), when "GOD shall be King over the whole earth; on that day shall GOD be one and His Name one" (Zechariah 14:9).

To summarize:

3	the future expansion of Israel	Israel is destined to expand over the whole world	consciousness of God's infinite light
2	the land promised to Abraham	the addition of the land of the three nations	super-conscious and conscious mind
1	the land conquered by Joshua	the land of the seven Canaanite nations	the seven emotions of the heart

[14] Cf. *Berachot* 6b; *Shirat Yisrael*, p. 156.

[15] *Sotah* 9b.

[16] Numbers 23:9.

[17] Proverbs 13:25.

[18] Psalms 37:16.

[19] *Avot* 4:1.

[20] *Ibid.* 5:10.

[21] *Bava Metzia* 38a.

[22] *Shabbat* 31a.

[23] This being the imagery in the parable of the Song of Songs.

[24] Isaiah 62:5.

[25] A settlement includes, of course, open land around it for agriculture.

[26] Song of Songs 3:10.

[27] The phrase, "a daughter of Jerusalem" (*bat Yerushalayim*) equals 988 = 52 times 19. 52 is the value of the word for "son" (*ben*) and 19 is the value of the name "Eve" (*Chavah*), the first woman. In mystical terms, every "daughter of Jerusalem," every settlement in the Land of Israel is married to a son of Eve, a (collective) soul of Israel.

[28] We saw above that "the Congregation of Israel" equals 26^2 and "the Land of Israel" equals 13 times 64 = 26 times 32. The difference between the two phrases, 156—6 times 26—is the value of the name Joseph (*Yosef*), the soul who represents in Kabbalah the secret of marital union, here, the marriage of the people to the land. Joseph (*Yosef*) equals Zion (*Tzion*, 156); he is the secret of true, Torah-oriented Zionism. (This implies that "You shall not commit adultery," as mentioned above).

Together, "the Congregation of Israel" and "the Land of Israel" equal 58 times 26. 58 is the value of the word for "grace" (*chen*). Thus, the union of the people to the land is the consummate revelation of "the grace of God." "Grace" in Hebrew implies "symmetry." And so, the union of the people to the land manifests Divine symmetry, which results from the union of the "direct," male light of the people settling the land and the "reflected," female light of the land bearing physical and spiritual fruit for the people.

[29] See the Rebbe's address of 13 Tishrei, 1977, quoted in *Karati VeEin Oneh*, pp. 148 ff.

[30] See *Malchut Yisrael*, vol. 1, pp. 265 ff.

[31] "There is no Torah like the Torah of the Land of Israel" (*Yalkut Shimoni*, Genesis 22).

[32] *Berachot* 8a.

[33] *Tikunei Zohar*, introduction, *s.v. Patach Eliahu*.

[34] In the Talmud, we are taught that in certain instances, "one should use his left hand to push away and his right hand to draw near" (*Sotah* 47a), implying that the *gevurah* of the left hand should precede the *chesed* of the right hand. The sages stated this rule in reference to the way that a mature educator/leader should relate to an immature student/follower. In order for the student to know the parameters of his or her limitations (thereby to have a sense of independence), the educator must first know how to gently "push away."

The "pushing away" itself must be in a context of love. First, therefore, one must evince a feeling of love and affinity with the other (in the idiom of Kabbalah, radiate an *or makif*—"all-encompassing light"—of *chesed*). Second, one can "push away" to give the other a correct sense of independence. And finally, one must "draw him near" with one's loving, benevolent right hand (in the idiom of Kabbalah, radiate an *or penimi*—"inner light"—of *chesed*).

All of this is said in relation to another individual. In our case, however, we are relating to two different parties. First, with our right hand of *chesed*, we bestow loving-kindness on our own people. Second, with our left hand of *gevurah*, we eliminate the terrorism of our enemies. And finally, after having achieved true peace (as we will describe), we will know which non-Jew we may accept as a "righteous gentile" and "resident alien."

[35] *Zohar* 1:16b.

[36] Midrash. See *Malchut Yisrael*, vol. 1, pp. 289 ff.

[37] This was the most complete expression of Nachshon's love for God (see *HaYom Yom*, 28 Nisan). Significantly, the numerical value of *Nachshon* (414) is the same as that of the words for "and you shall love" (*veahavta*), that appears both in the commandment to love God ("and you shall love GOD, your God" [Deuteronomy 6:5]) and the commandment to love one's fellow Jew ("and you shall love your neighbor as yourself" [Leviticus 19:18]).

[38] "The beginning of defeat is retreat" (*Sotah* 44b).

[39] In the Rebbe's words: "Of course, I cannot in any way debate with those who believe that the Arabs have legitimate cause to demand the ceding of the territories that belong to them, for we have no common denominator from which to proceed. But they must certainly remember that if the Arabs have a legitimate claim on the territories [they possessed] before '67, they have the same legitimate claim to the Old City [of Jerusalem], as well as to Tel

Aviv, Hadera, and all of 'Palestine'" (Letter of 13 Shevat, 5741 [1981] to Mr. Pinchus M. Kalms, London).

[40] This extremist approach recalls that of the zealots (*biryonim*) of Second Temple times. See *Gitin* 56a ff.

[41] *Tanya*, chapter 13.

[42] See *Igeret HaKodesh* 8 (113a).

[43] Politics in general is an invention of people living in the desert, who are subject to the illusions of false mirages. The first politician, the first person in the Torah to rally people around a "party line" (in the name of democracy, of course) was Korah. Korah began his rebellion only after God had decreed that the Jews would have to wander in the desert for forty years.

[44] The *sefirot* of each world develop into *partzufim* ("persona"):

- *chochmah* becomes the *partzuf* of *Abba* ("father"),
- *binah* becomes the *partzuf* of *Ima* ("mother"),
- the six *sefirot* from *chesed* to *yesod* become the *partzuf* of *Z'eir Anpin* (the "small countenance," the son of *Abba* and *Ima* and bridegroom of the following *partzuf*), and
- *malchut* becomes the *partzuf* of *Nukva diZ'eir Anpin* (the "female of the small countenance," the daughter of *Abba* and *Ima* and bride of *Z'eir Anpin*).

These four *partzufim* correspond to the four letters of the Name *Havayah*, which in turn correspond to the four spiritual worlds of *Atzilut, Beriah, Yetzirah*, and *Asiyah*.

(There is a higher, fifth element in each of these sets of four: the *sefirah* of *keter*, which develops into the *partzuf* of *Arich Anpin* [the "long countenance"]; the tip of the *yud*; and the world of *Adam Kadmon* ["primordial man"].)

Of the four *partzufim, Abba* and *Z'eir Anpin* are male and *Ima* and *Nukva* are female. Thus, the two letters *yud* and *vav* embody the "male" energy of the Name *Havayah* and the two letters *hei* embody its "female" energy. By association, then, *Atzilut* and

Yetzirah are relatively "male" worlds while *Beriah* and *Asiyah* are "female" worlds. (*Arich Anpin* is considered androgynous in this context; its "right side" is male and its "left side" is female. From yet a higher perspective, its left side itself is right: "there is no left in that *Atika* ["Ancient One," a connotation for the *partzuf* of *keter*], all [i.e., both right and left] is right" [*Zohar* 3:129a].)

The four worlds, the four letters, and the four *partzufim* are thus each seen as comprising a higher and lower "couple." Inasmuch as the male is associated with the right and the female with the left, each group of four contains a higher and lower left and right.

keter	*Arich Anpin*	tip of *yud*	*Adam Kadmon*	"all is right"
chochmah	*Abba*	*yud*	*Atzilut*	higher right
binah	*Ima*	*hei*	*Beriah*	higher left
chesed to *yesod*	*Z'eir Anpin*	*vav*	*Yetzirah*	lower right
malchut	*Nukva diZ'eir Anpin*	*hei*	*Asiyah*	lower left

Chapter Nine

[1] If it is necessary to enter foreign countries in order to purge terrorism directed against Israel (or the Jewish people in the Diaspora), we must do so without hesitation.

[2] "If someone threatens your life [literally, 'comes to kill you'], be first to kill him" (*Berachot* 58a).

[3] The numerical value of "might" (*gevurah*, 216) is the same as that of "fear" (*yirah*).

[4] See the Rebbe's audience with Rabbi Efraim Eliezer Yalles on *Chol HaMo'ed* Pesach, 1983, quoted in *Karati VeEin Oneh*, pp. 700 ff.

[5] *Ketubot* 26b.

[6] Isaiah 5:7.

[7] Address of *Shabbat Re'ei*, 1978, quoted in *Karati VeEin Oneh*, pp. 231 ff.

[8] *Orach Chaim* 329, which enjoins us to defend ourselves against would-be invaders even on *Shabbat*.

[9] Letter of 27 Kislev, 5741 [1980] to Mr. Pinchus M. Kalms, London.

[10] *Berachot* 33a.

[11] Deuteronomy 32:43.

[12] Another instance of vengeance that the Torah views positively is the act of Phineas (Numbers 25).

Chapter Ten

[1] *Tana d'vei Eliyahu Rabbah* 1. This principle is derived from the phrase in the beginning of the Torah, "the way to the Tree of Life." The sages interpret "the way" to refer to "the way of the land," and "the Tree of Life" to refer to the Torah. From this it is clear that the way of the land not only must precede the Torah chronologically, but that it is the (one and only) way *to* the Torah. Settling the land and uprooting terrorism is the one and only way to create the environment necessary for the people to begin to live in accordance with the Torah in the Promised Land. Only when we have successfully accomplished the first two steps of our program can we plant in our land (the consciousness of) the Tree of Life.

[2] Micah 7:20.

[3] Genesis 31:42. Isaac is depicted in the *Zohar* (3:219a, in *Ra'aya Mehemna*) as the force that combats the Arabs. See R. Dovber of Lubavtich, *Sha'arei Teshuvah* 85c.

[4] Genesis 25:27; Rashi *ad loc.*

[5] *Tikunei Zohar*, introduction.

[6] Proverbs 29:4.

[7] *Tikunei Zohar*, introduction, *s.v. Patach Eliayhu*: "Justice [מֹשְׁפֵּט] is the middle axis...it is mercy." The preceding statement, "Law [דִּין] is *gevurah*," refers to the strict letter of the law before taking real-life situations into consideration.

[8] Modern-day Israeli law is a hodgepodge of Turkish, British, and Jewish law; Jewish law *per se* is relegated to rabbinic courts that are authorized to deal with "religious" issues (marriage, divorce, etc.) alone. The fact that Jewish law is accorded secondary status relative to the secular legal system denigrates it and makes it difficult for the rabbinic judges to apply it with its true,

characteristic compassion—even in those spheres over which it has been granted authority.

Furthermore, this denigration of Jewish law influences the attitude of non-religious Jews in Israel. They naturally question why they should submit to the dictates of Jewish law when the very system that forces them to do so does not truly respect it. Obviously, this creates friction between them and the rabbinic court system, making it even more difficult for the latter to implement Jewish law with its characteristic compassion. The sages teach us (*Berachot* 33a) that it is impossible to express compassion to someone who lacks *da'at*, which in this case means to someone who does not respect Jewish law.

[9] Lamentations 2:1.

[10] 3:16.

[11] *Ketubot* 9:2.

[12] This is the inner power of the Torah's monetary laws, which unite all the tribes (or present-day communities) of Israel. The tribes were united symbolically in the gems of the breastplate worn over the High Priest's heart—the "breastplate of judgment" (Exodus 28:15)—the epitome of the "beauty of Israel."

The Code of Jewish Law is divided into four books. The book that deals with civil law is called "the breastplate of judgment." It is noteworthy that most of the content of Jewish civil law applies to non-Jews as well as to Jews. Thus, the beauty of Jewish law, pertinent as it is to the non-Jewish world, is meant to shine its light to non-Jews and attract them to seek true justice in Jewish courts, encouraging them to become righteous gentiles by committing themselves to observe all of the seven commandments given by God, in the Torah, to non-Jews.

Chapter Eleven

[1] Indeed, the sages teach that the Land of Israel is higher than all other lands (*Zevachim* 54b).

[2] *Sefer Yetzirah* 1:5.

[3] Psalms 116:9.

[4] As in למנצח, "for the conductor" (Psalms 4:1, etc.).

[5] Together with the hundreds of thousands of Jews who have returned to Israel from Russia, there is also a large percentage of non-Jews. This has to a certain extent tainted the positive effect that this immigration would have had on society in Israel as a whole had it been truly Jewish. In addition, the drive that has motivated part of this immigration is yet another example of fleeing from the perils and trauma of exile, rather than experiencing the true elevation of consciousness that comes with the experience of victory, the true ascent to the Land of Israel.

[6] To leave a life of physical prosperity and security to come to Israel, the Promised Land, entails the uplifting (i.e., sense of *netzach*) of one's Jewish consciousness, so that one will come to recognize and desire the eternal, Divine values of the Torah.

[7] Psalms 126:1.

[8] For this reason (see chapter 2, endnote 7), the Rebbe did not encourage mass, world-wide *aliyah*, for the time is not yet ripe.

[9] The word for "loving-kindness," *chesed*, is composed of three letters, *chet*, *samech*, and *dalet*. When the word is "generated" by progressive repetition—*chet*, *chet samech*, *chet samech dalet*—its numerical value (148) equals that of *netzach* ("victory"). This is an allusion in Kabbalah that *netzach* is the extension of *chesed*.

[10] See endnote 3 of this chapter. The Rebbe teaches that in our days, "Assyria" (from the word *osher*, "prosperity") refers to

affluent societies (such as the United States) and "Egypt" (from the word *meitzar*, "straits") refers to dictatorial regimes (such as communist Russia).

[11] In Kabbalah, *netzach* and *hod* correspond to the two legs, while *yesod* corresponds to the reproductive organ and *malchut* to the crown of the reproductive organ. Inasmuch as the legs extend below the reproductive organ, the stages of the redemptive process corresponding to *netzach* and *hod* continue to occur—and reach their completion—after the subsequent stages corresponding to *yesod* and *malchut*. Thus, mass *aliyah* continues and is completed only after the final stages of the redemptive process. The continuation of *hod* is the fulfillment of the verse, "For then will I make the nations pure of speech, so that they will all call upon the Name of GOD, to serve Him together" (Zephaniah 3:9).

Chapter Twelve

[1] *Zohar* 3:236a.

[2] In Kabbalah, these two *sefirot* share a common Divine Name, *Tzevakot* ("Hosts"). In particular, the Divine Name that corresponds to *netzach* is the combined form *Havayah Tzevakot* and the Divine Name that corresponds to *hod* is the combined form *Elokim Tzevakot*. In *netzach*, this Name brings the Jewish people— "GOD's hosts" (*tzivot HaShem*, Exodus 12:41)—to the Promised Land. In *hod*, this very Name drives foreign elements—harmful invaders in the land of the true hosts—out of the land.

When the letters of the Name *Tzevakot* are transformed by the process known as *atbash*, the result is a Name whose root means "partner" (*shutaf*). This implies both that the two *sefirot* of *netzach* and *hod* must function together as "partners" (for every stride the right foot takes to promote Jewish immigration to Israel, so does the left foot take an equal and opposite stride to reject undesirable elements from the land) and that God and the Jewish people must act as "partners," as it were, in order to realize the tasks of *netzach* and *hod*. With our own two feet firmly on the ground, we must walk together with God, in total commitment to fulfill His will— that His chosen people inherit His chosen land and allow no adulterer to defile the holy marriage of the people to the land.

[3] *Bava Kama* 2b.

[4] The correspondences of the body's physiological systems to the supernal *sefirot* and powers of the soul are explained in our upcoming book, *The Spirit of Life: Kabbalah and Medicine*.

[5] Leviticus 8:28, 20:22.

[6] According to Maimonides (*Mishneh Torah*, *Avodat Kochavim* 10:6), "righteous gentiles" are permitted to live in the Land of Israel when the observance of the Jubilee year is renewed. With

regard to righteous gentiles in general, and the obligation of knowledgeable Jews to teach non-Jews to observe their commandments, see our upcoming book, *Jews and Non-Jews: Creating a World to Serve God Together*. Although this obligation existed since the Torah was given (*Mishneh Torah, Melachim* 8:10), it was not implemented in prior generations because the religious bias of non-Jewish governments made doing so a capital crime. Now that this impediment has been lifted, we are free to fulfill this obligation. Anti-Semitism, of course, still exists, but as with all forms of darkness, it is best combated by disseminating light, in this case, the Torah's vision of the non-Jew's role in rectifying reality.

[7] Channeling government funds to hostile, non-Jewish elements happens now at the expense of providing the Jewish poor with the welfare and social benefits that they rightly deserve; this most unfortunately occurs over and over again in modern Israel (see the Rebbe's addresses of *Shabbat Bamidbar* and *Shabbat Naso*, 1973, quoted in *Karati VeEin Oneh*, pp. 30 ff).

[8] *Mishneh Torah, Matnot Ani'im* 7:1.

[9] *Vayikra Rabbah* 17:6.

[10] Significantly, the first city in the Land of Israel that was conquered by war—in the time of the patriarchs—was the city of Shechem (conquered by Shimon and Levi, two sons of Jacob). In Kabbalah, this city is identified with the attribute of *yesod*, for which reason Jacob—asserting that he had conquered the city "with my sword and bow" (Genesis 48:22)—gave the city to his son, Joseph.

[11] Genesis 30:24.

[12] In the Torah, the complete defeat of the enemies of Israel comes with the annihilation of Amalek, the fulfillment of the commandment, "You shall wipe out the memory of Amalek from under the heavens, do not forget!" (Deuteronomy 25:19).

Wiping out the seed of Amalek is the second of the three commandments that the Jewish people are commanded to perform upon entering the Land of Israel: (1) to appoint a king, (2) to wipe out the seed of Amalek, and (3) to build the Temple (*Mishneh Torah, Melachim* 1:1).

Fighting the wars against the enemies of Israel relates in particular to the Messiah descended from Joseph. The prophet states that the house of Esau—including the seed of Amalek, Esau's grandson—will be burnt only by the house of Joseph (Obadiah 1:18). Nonetheless, the complete annihilation of Amalek, the annihilation of his very "memory" from Jewish consciousness, will be accomplished by the Davidic Messiah, by the spirit of the Messiah descended from Joseph that will incarnate in him. Thus, all three commandments refer to the Davidic Messiah (and therefore Maimonides, in his discussion of these commandments, does not mention the Messiah descended from Joseph at all).

The two promises of the complete Ingathering of the Exiles and the transformation of all peoples on earth to worship the God of Israel together follow the three commandments as stated by Maimonides.

As we have explained elsewhere at length, these five phases correspond to the five levels of the soul of the Messiah himself in ascending order:

yechidah	transformation of humanity
chayah	Ingathering of the Exiles
neshamah	building the Temple
ruach	annihilation of Amalek
nefesh	appointing a king

[13] Ecclesiastes 3:8.

[14] 4:2.

Chapter Thirteen

[1] In Kabbalah, promises, both to others and to oneself, are associated with the soul's two previous powers of *netzach* and *hod*. The attribute of *yesod* is the driving force of the soul to make the promises of *netzach* and *hod* come true in external reality—*malchut* ("kingdom"), the culmination of the rectification process.

The deep sense of satisfaction and joy that comes with fulfilling one's dreams and promises in external reality—in Kabbalah the union of *yesod* and *malchut*—resembles that which comes with the consummation of marital relations. Indeed, the union of *yesod* and *malchut* is portrayed in Kabbalah as the union of groom and bride.

The ultimate union of *yesod* and *malchut* is the culmination of the entire rectification process. When it is consummated, we will witness our dream of creating for God a dwelling place on earth come true. We will presently explain that within the stage of *yesod* itself there is also a phenomenon of union, that of the higher, "male waters" of the Torah and the lower, "female waters" of secular science. Relative to the ultimate union of *yesod* and *malchut*, the union that takes places within the domain of *yesod* itself is the union of the male and female components within the male himself.

The union of Divine, God-given wisdom (the wisdom of the Torah) and of secular, human wisdom (the wisdom of science) takes place in the human mind, which, in the emotive attributes of the heart is reflected in the attribute of *yesod*, whose inner essence is truth. (Intellectual truth reflects itself in emotive truth, the drive to verify, which itself is the motivating force behind the empirically based scientific method.) The final, ultimate union takes place in the domain of external reality itself—*malchut* (with *yesod* joined to it). At this, final stage, the physical world itself becomes a dwelling place for God—"And GOD shall be king over the whole earth; on that day GOD shall be one and His Name one" (Zechariah 14:9).

² As stated above and as will be explained below, this is a property intrinsic to the soul-root of Joseph, the dreamer and dream interpreter (see *Transforming Darkness into Light*, pp. 102-103).

³ *Mishneh Torah, Melachim* 12:4.

⁴ *Chagigah* 19b. The Ba'al Shem Tov teaches that there are three stages of Divine service: "submission," "separation," and "sweetening" (*Keter Shem Tov* 28). In the stage of submission, one learns, by suppressing one's ego, to clearly identify and distinguish in one's own psyche the holy from the secular. The actual separation of the secular from the holy, allowing the holy to manifest itself in full, occurs in the second stage, separation. The third stage, sweetening, begins when the soul becomes sufficiently strong, having identified itself purely with the holy, to shine its light into the realm of the secular and sanctify it. This mirrors the process of transforming darkness into light described in the beginning of our discussion.

⁵ *Zohar* 1:117a. This image is taken from the Torah's account of the flood (see *Awakening the Spark Within*, pp. 2 ff; *Transforming Darkness into Light*, p. xiii).

⁶ This is the beginning of the fulfillment of Isaiah's prophecy: "The earth will be filled with the knowledge of GOD like water covers the seabed" (Isaiah 11:9).

⁷ *Avot* 3:17.

⁸ Exodus 19:20.

⁹ *Shabbat* 88b.

¹⁰ *Ibid.* 105a.

¹¹ Proverbs 3:6.

¹² *Zohar* 3:233b.

¹³ *Yoma* 8:9.

¹⁴ *Sanhedrin* 110a.

Chapter Fourteen

[1] In the words of Kabbalah: "All returning [i.e., reflected] light returns to its ultimate, primordial source [i.e., above the revealed source of straight/direct light]." Kabbalah sees in the story of Jonathan and David one of the most outstanding examples in the Bible of the relationship of straight/direct light to returning, reflected light. Jonathan shines direct light to David by willfully and lovingly relinquishing the kingdom to him, and David returns his love so intensely that the Bible testifies that David "surpassed" Jonathan (1 Samuel 20:41). That David surpassed Jonathan signifies that David's returning light (his sense of gratitude and love for his companion) returned so high that it reached the infinite source of all light in God's very essence, above the revealed, conscious source of Jonathan's own devotion for David.

[2] *Chagigah* 14b; Psalms 101:7.

[3] In Hebrew, the word for "water"—*mayim*—is in the plural (or "dual") form, implying that in every body of water, even the smallest drop, there are in fact two facets/dimensions of water. This alludes to the reflection of the consummate union of the higher waters and the lower waters in every single drop of water.

Additionally, *mayim*—spelled *mem-yud-mem*—is symmetric, that is, identical, whether read from beginning to end or from end to beginning. In Kabbalah, *mayim* is the symmetric form of the word for "who?"—*mi*—spelled *mem-yud*, alluding to the verse, "Lift up your eyes and see *Who* [*mi*] created these" (Isaiah 40:26). Every drop of water reflects the secret of "Who created these," for in every drop of water the higher waters meet the lower waters to create, in perfect union, new forms of life.

In the creative process, it is the very same Divine "Who" that descends as the higher waters (alluded to in the first and second letters of *mayim*) and ascends as the lower waters (alluded to in the second and third letters of *mayim*) to create new life. (The union takes place in the *yud*, the middle letter of *mayim*, the point common to both the higher manifestation of "Who" and to the lower manifestation of "Who," their axis of symmetry.)

In Kabbalah, the soul of Moses, whose name means "I have drawn him from the water" (Exodus 2:10), represents the consciousness of the perfect union of the higher and lower waters. "Water" symbolizes the Torah—"the Torah of Moses" (Malachi 3:22)—as it is said, "There is no 'water' but Torah" (*Bava Kama* 82a). Of this Divine state of consciousness, it is said that the Messiah the son of David will in fact possess the soul of Moses, for "He is the first redeemer and he is the last redeemer" (*Shemot Rabbah* 4:2).

In the "progressive numbering system" (*mispar kidmi*, in which every letter is calculated as the sum of the values of all the letters from *alef* to, and including, that letter), *mayim* (*mem* = 145, *yud* = 55, *mem* = 145) equals Moses (345). Moreover, the simple numerical value of *mayim*, 90, is two times 45, the value of the word for "what" (*mah*), implying a state of true selflessness, the most essential characteristic of Moses, who stated twice (in reference to himself and his brother, Aaron), "we are what [i.e., 'nothing']" (Exodus 16:7-8).

Thus, we see that water represents the union of two manifestations of "who" and two states of "what." The two states of "what" correspond to the two manifestations of "who": The male dimension of the higher waters (present in every drop of water) possesses its inherent state of selflessness, in descending from on high—*giving itself over* to unite with the lower waters; and the female dimension of the lower waters possesses its inherent state of selflessness in ascending—*rising up and out of itself*—to unite with the higher waters.

[4] Zephaniah 3:9.

[5] See Maimonides' *Commentary on the Mishnah, Sanhedrin* 10.

[6] *Zohar* 3:75a; *Tanya,* chapter 34.

[7] Genesis 1:28. Procreation is known as the "great commandment" (*Tosafot, Gitin* 38a, *s.v. Kol HaMeshachrer*).

[8] Deuteronomy 28:47.

[9] Isaiah 2:2-3.

Chapter Fifteen

[1] On Exodus 25:32.

[2] p. 171.

[3] 1 Kings 6:4; see *Menachot* 86b.

[4] Isaiah 5:20. Maimonides reads this verse as referring to people of tainted, unrectified character traits, whom he calls spiritually sick (*Mishneh Torah*, *Deiot* 2:1). This "leftist" perversion of light and darkness characterized the Hellenist trend in the Second Commonwealth of Israel. This led to war and the miracle of Chanukah—the victory of true Judaism over Hellenism as most profoundly expressed by the miracle of the *menorah*, which we commemorate to this day.

The people whom Isaiah rebukes first "say evil is good...put darkness for light and...bitter for sweet," meaning that they first believe in the greatness ("enlightenment") of non-Jewish culture. This leads them to "say good is evil, etc.," to consider Jewish culture inferior. The source of this belief in the superiority of non-Jewish culture is a deep-seated inferiority complex relative to the non-Jew, as the Rebbe repeatedly stated.

[5] *Bava Batra* 25a.

[6] Numbers 8:2.

[7] *Menachot* 86b.

[8] In addition to this condition, according to certain opinions in Jewish law, we are forbidden under solemn oath to initiate a process of mass immigration to Israel before the time of redemption comes (based on *Midrash Tanchuma*, *Devarim* 4). When the time is ripe, however, God will signal us that He has nullified the oath, in the form of Diaspora Jewry's spontaneous arousal to immigrate to the Land of Israel, which will occur once the country becomes authentically Jewish. According to other opinions, the

oath was nullified long ago, for the non-Jews have not kept their side of the promise upon which the oath was made, not to overly oppress the Jews exiled in their lands.

Similarly, inasmuch as the Arabs in our days break their word time after time, we are under no obligation to keep our side of the "peace accords" with them.

[9] Proverbs 10:25.

[10] *Sha'ar HaYichud VehaEmunah*, chapter 5 (79b-80a).

[11] *Vayikra Rabbah* 29:11.

[12] *Zohar* 1:181a.

[13] As he said, "I will be lowly in my own eyes" (2 Samuel 6:22).

[14] Ecclesiastes 1:7.

[15] Exodus 25:36.

[16] Zechariah 14:9.

Glossary

Note: all foreign terms are Hebrew unless otherwise indicated. Terms preceded by an asterisk have their own entries.

Abba (אבא, "father" [Aramaic]): the *partzuf* of *chochmah.

Adam Kadmon (אדם קדמון, "primordial man"): the first *world.

Arich Anpin (אריך אנפין, "the long face" or "the infinitely patient one"): the external *partzuf* of *keter (the inner dimension is *Atik Yomin). In psychological terms, it is synonymous with will. It possesses its own *keter* (the *gulgalta*), and its own *chochmah (*mocha stima'ah).

Asiyah (עשיה, "action"): the lowest of the four *worlds.

Atbash: (אתב״ש): the simple reflective transformation. The first letter of the alphabet is paired with the last, the second with the second-to-last, and so on. The letters of these pairs may then be interchanged.

כ	י	ט	ח	ז	ו	ה	ד	ג	ב	א
ל	מ	נ	ס	ע	פ	צ	ק	ר	ש	ת

Atik: short for *Atik Yomin.

Atik Yomin (עתיק יומין, "the ancient of days" [Aramaic]): the inner *partzuf* of *keter.

Atika Kadisha (עתיקא קדישא, "the holy ancient One" [Aramaic]): in some contexts, this term is a synonym for *Atik Yomin*; in others, for *keter in general.

Atzilut (אצילות, "Emanation"): First and highest of the four *worlds emanating from *Adam Kadmon*.

Av (אב, "father"): the fifth month of the Jewish calendar.

Ba'al Shem Tov (בעל שם טוב, "Master of the Good Name [of God]"): Title of Rabbi Yisrael ben Eliezer (1698-1760), founder of the Chassidic movement (*Chassidut*).

Ba'al Teshuvah (בעל תשובה, "one who returns"): one who returns to the ways of Judaism and adherence to Jewish law after a period of estrangement. Often used in contrast to a *tzadik*, who has not undergone such a period. The *ba'al teshuvah* strives continually to ascend, return and become subsumed within God's essence; the *tzadik* strives primarily to serve God by doing good deeds and thus drawing His light into the world. Ideally these two paths are meant to be inter-included, i.e. that every Jew should embody both the service of the *ba'al teshuvah* and that of the *tzadik*, as well. See also *teshuvah*.

Beriah (בריאה, "creation"): the second of the four *worlds.

Binah (בינה, "understanding"): the third of the ten *sefirot*.

Birur (בירור, "separation," "choosing," or "refinement"): a type of *tikun* in which one must work to separate good from evil in any given entity, and then reject the evil and accept the good. This may be done actively or in one's consciousness. See *yichud*.

Bitachon (בטחון, "confidence"): 1. the feeling of confidence in one's God-given power to take initiative and succeed in one's mission in life. See *emunah*. 2. The inner experience of the *sefirah* of *netzach*. 3. ("trust"): the feeling that God will orchestrate events in accord with the greatest revealed good. This passive *bitachon* is associated with the *sefirah* of *hod*.

Bitul (בטול, "selflessness"): any of a number of states of selflessness or self-abnegation. The inner experience of the *sefirah* of *chochmah*.

Chabad (חב״ד), acronym for **chochmah, *binah, *da'at* (חכמה בינה דעת, "wisdom, understanding, knowledge"): 1. the first triad of **sefirot*, which constitute the intellect (see *Chagat, Nehi*). 2. the branch of **Chassidut* founded by Rabbi Shneur Zalman of Liadi (1745-1812), emphasizing the role of the intellect and meditation in the service of God.

Chagat (חג״ת), acronym for **chesed, *gevurah, *tiferet* (חסד גבורה תפארת, "loving-kindness, strength, beauty"): the second triad of **sefirot*, which together constitute the primary emotions (see *Chabad, Nehi*).

Chasadim: plural of **chesed* (second sense).

Chayah (חיה, "living one"): the second highest of the five levels of the **soul.

Chesed (חסד, "loving-kindness"; pl. חסדים, *chasadim*): 1. the fourth of the ten **sefirot*. 2. a manifestation of this attribute, specifically in **da'at*.

Chochmah (חכמה, "wisdom" or "insight"): the second of the ten **sefirot*.

Da'at (דעת, "knowledge"): 1. the unifying force within the ten **sefirot*. 2. the third *sefirah* of the intellect, counted as one of the ten *sefirot* when *keter*, the superconscious, is not counted.

Din (דין, "judgment"; pl. דינים, *dinim*): 1. a synonym for **gevurah*. 2. a manifestation of this attribute. 3. a synonym for **kal vechomer*.

Emunah (אמונה, "faith" or "belief"): 1. the belief in the existence of God. 2. the belief that no matter what God does, it is all ultimately for the greatest good, even if it does not appear so to us presently. See **bitachon*. 3. the inner experience associated with **reisha d'lo ityada*.

Gedulah (גדלה, "greatness"): a synonym for **chesed*.

Gematria (גימטריא, "numerology" [Aramaic]): The technique of comparing Hebrew words and phrases based on their numerical values.

Gevurah (גבורה, "power" or "strength"; pl. גבורות, *gevurot*): 1. the fifth of the ten **sefirot*. 2. a manifestation of this attribute, specifically in **da'at*.

Gevurot: plural of **gevurah* (second sense).

Gulgalta (גלגלתא, "the skull" [Aramaic]): the **keter* of **Arich Anpin*. In psychological terms, the interface between pleasure and will, which serves as the origin of the super-conscious will.

Halachah (הלכה, "way" or "walking"): 1. the entire corpus of Jewish law. 2. a specific Jewish law.

Hassidism (חסידות, *Chassidut*, "piety" or "loving-kindness"): 1. An attribute or way of life that goes beyond the letter of the law. 2. The movement within Judaism founded by Rabbi Yisrael Ba'al Shem Tov (1648-1760), the purpose of which is to awaken the Jewish people to its own inner self through the inner dimension of the Torah and thus to prepare the way for the advent of **Mashiach*. 3. The oral and written teachings of this movement.

Havayah (יהו־ה), also known as the Tetragrammaton ("four-letter Name"). Due to its great sanctity, this Name may only be pronounced in the Holy Temple, and its correct pronunciation is not known today. When one is reciting a complete Scriptural verse or liturgy, it is read as if it were the Name *Adni*; otherwise one says *Hashem* (השם, "the Name") or *Havayah* (הויה, a permutation of the four letters of this Name).

Havayah is the most sacred of God's Names. Although no name can fully express God's essence, the Name *Havayah* in certain contexts *refers* to God's essence. In these cases it is called "the higher Name *Havayah*" and is termed "the essential Name" (שם העצם), "the unique Name" (שם המיוחד), and "the explicit Name" (שם המפורש).

Otherwise, the Name Havayah refers to God as He manifests Himself through creation. In these cases it is called "the lower Name Havayah," and its four letters are seen to depict in their form the creative process and allude to the worlds, ten sefirot, etc., as follows:

		creation	worlds	sefirot
קוצו של י	upper "tip" of the *yud*	will to create	*Adam Kadmon*	*keter*
י	*yud*	contraction	*Atzilut*	*chochmah*
ה	*hei*	expansion	*Beriah*	*binah*
ו	*vav*	extension	*Yetzirah*	the six *midot*
ה	*hei*	expansion	*Asiyah*	*malchut*

The lower Name *Havayah* appears on several levels. It is first manifest as the light within all the *sefirot*. It thus possesses on this level ten iterations, which are indicated as ten vocalizations—each using one of the ten vowels. (These are only meditative "vocalizations," since it is forbidden to pronounce the Name *Havayah* with any vocalization, as we have said.) For example, when each of its four letters is vocalized with a *kamatz*, it signifies the light within the *sefirah* of *keter*; when they are each vocalized with a *patach*, it signifies the light within the *sefirah* of *chochmah*. The other Names of God (including the subsequent manifestations of the Name *Havayah*) refer to the vessels of the *sefirot*. In the world of *Atzilut*, where these Names are principally manifest, both the vessels and the lights of the *sefirot* are manifestations of Divinity.

The second manifestation of the lower Name *Havayah* is as the life-force and creative energy of the *sefirah* of *chochmah*. (This is alluded to in the verse, "*Havayah* in *chochmah* founded the earth" [Proverbs 3:19].)

Its third manifestation is as the vessel of the *sefirah* of *binah*. This manifestation is indicated by the consonants of the Name vocalized with the vowels of (and read as) the Name *Elokim* (for example, Deuteronomy 3:24, etc.).

The most basic manifestation of the lower Name *Havayah* is in the vessel of the *sefirah* of *tiferet*, whose inner experience is mercy. The Name *Havayah* in general is associated with "the principle of mercy," since mercy is the most basic emotion through which God relates to His creation.

Hod (הוד, "splendor," "thanksgiving," "acknowledgment"): the eighth of the ten *sefirot.

Ima (אמא, "mother" [Aramaic]): the *partzuf of *binah.

Kabbalah (קבלה, "receiving" or "tradition"): the esoteric dimension of the Torah.

Kabbalat Shabbat (קבלת שבת, "welcoming the Sabbath"): the series of psalms and hymns, etc. recited as a prelude to the Friday night prayer service, to mark the onset of the Sabbath.

Kav (קו, "line"): the ray of light beamed into the vacated space created in consequence of the *tzimtzum.

Keter (כתר, "crown"): the first of the ten *sefirot.

Lecha Dodi (לכה דודי, "Come, my beloved"): a hymn recited as part of *Kabbalat Shabbat.

Lights: see *Sefirah*.

Lubavitch (ליובאוויטש, "City of Love" [Russian]): the town that served as the center of the *Chabad movement from 1812 to 1915; the movement became known also after the name of this town.

Malchut (מלכות, "kingdom"): the last of the ten *sefirot.

Mashiach (משיח, "anointed one," "Messiah"): the prophesied descendant of King David who will reinstate the Torah-ordained monarchy (which he will head), rebuild the Holy

*Temple, and gather the exiled Jewish people to their homeland. This series of events (collectively called "the Redemption") will usher in an era of eternal, universal peace and true knowledge of God, called "the messianic era." There is also a prophesied messianic figure called *Mashiach ben* Joseph, who will rectify certain aspects of reality in preparation for the advent of *Mashiach ben* David.

Mazal (מזל, pl. מזלות, *mazalot*): 1. a spiritual conduit of Divine beneficence (from the root נזל, "to flow"). 2. specifically, the thirteen tufts of the "beard" of *Arich Anpin*. 3. a physical embodiment of such a spiritual conduit, such as a star, planet, constellation, etc. 4. specifically, the twelve constellations of the zodiac. 5. According to our sages, the Jewish people are not under the influence of the *mazalot* (*Shabbat* 156a). The Ba'al Shem Tov teaches that the Divine "nothingness" itself is the true *mazal* of the Jewish people.

Menorah (מנורה, "candelabrum"): the seven-branched candelabrum that was lit daily in the sanctuary of the *Tabernacle and, afterwards, in the Holy *Temple.

Midah (מדה, "measure" or "attribute," pl. מדות, *midot*): 1. an attribute of God. 2. specifically, one of the *sefirot* from *chesed* to *malchut*, in contrast to the higher *sefirot* of the intellect. 3. one of the thirteen attributes of mercy, which are part of the revelation of *keter*.

Midot: plural of *midah*.

Midrash (מדרש, "seeking"; pl. מדרשים, Midrashim): the second major body of the oral Torah (after the *Talmud), consisting of halachic or homiletic material couched as linguistic analyses of the Biblical text. An individual work of midrashic material is also called a Midrash; a specific analysis is called a midrash.

The Midrash is a corpus of many works written over the span of several centuries (roughly the second to the eighth CE), mostly in the Holy Land. The chief collection of homiletic midrashic material is the *Rabbah* ("great") series, covering the five books of Moses and the five scrolls. Other important collections are *Midrash Tanchuma*, *Midrash Tehilim*, *Pesikta d'Rav Kahana*, *Pirkei d'Rabbi Eliezer* and *Tana d'vei Eliahu*. Several later collections contain material that has reached us in its original form. These include *Midrash HaGadol* and *Yalkut Shimoni*. There are many smaller, minor Midrashim, as well; some of these are to be found in the collection *Otzar HaMidrashim*. Halachic Midrashim include the *Mechilta*, the *Sifra* and the *Sifrei*.

Mitzvah (מצוה, "commandment"; pl. מצות, *mitzvot*): one of the six hundred thirteen commandments given by God to the Jewish people, or seven commandments given by God to the nations of the world, at Mt. Sinai. 2. one of the seven commandments instituted by the sages. 3. idiomatically, any good deed.

Mocha Stima'ah (מוחא סתימאה, "the hidden brain" [Aramaic]): the *chochmah* of *Arich Anpin*. In psychological terms, the power to generate new insight (כח המשכיל).

Mochin d'Abba (מוחין דאבא, "brains of *Abba*" [Aramaic]): a state of consciousness, mentality, or cognitive life-force in which one experiences *chochmah*, or insight.

Mochin d'Ima (מוחין דאמא, "brains of *Ima*" [Aramaic]): a state of consciousness or mentality, or cognitive life-force in which one experiences *binah*, or understanding or rationality.

Motzaei Shabbat (מוצאי שבת, "the outgoings of the Sabbath"): the night after the termination of *Shabbat; Saturday night.

Nefesh (נפש, "creature," "soul"): 1. the soul in general. 2. the lowest of the five levels of the *soul.

Nehi (נה"י), acronym for *netzach, *hod, *yesod (נצח הוד יסוד, "victory, splendor, foundation"): the third triad of *sefirot,

which together constitute the attributes of behavior (see
Chabad, *Chagat*).

Nekudim (נקודים, "dotted," "spotted"): the second stage in the
development of the *world of *Atzilut*.

Neshamah (נשמה, "soul"): 1. the soul in general. 2. the third of
the five levels of the *soul.

Netzach (נצח, "victory," "eternity"): the seventh of the ten *sefirot*.

Notrikun (נוטריקון, "acronym"): a method of interpretation in
which a word is seen as comprising the initials or main
consonantal letters of another word or phrase.

Nukvei d'Z'eir Anpin (נוקביה דזעיר אנפין [Aramaic]): the
partzuf of *malchut*.

Omer: see *Sefirat HaOmer*.

Partzuf (פרצוף, "persona"; pl. פרצופים, *partzufim*): the third and
final stage in the development of a *sefirah*, in which it
metamorphoses from a tenfold articulation of sub-*sefirot* into a
human-like figure possessing the full set of intellectual and
emotional powers. As such, it may thus interact with the other
partzufim (which could not occur before this transformation.
This stage of development constitutes the transition from
Tohu to *Tikun* (or from *Nekudim* to *Berudim*, see under
Worlds).

The *sefirot* develop into a primary and a secondary array of
partzufim, as follows:

sefirah	primary *partzufim*		secondary *partzufim*	
keter	עתיק יומין *Atik Yomin*	"The Ancient of Days"	עתיק יומין *Atik Yomin*	[The male dimension of] "the Ancient of Days"
			נוקביה דעתיק יומין *Nukvei* *d'Atik Yomin*	[The female dimension of] "the Ancient of Days"
	אריך אנפין *Arich Anpin*	"The Long Face"	אריך אנפין *Arich Anpin*	[The male dimension of] "the Long Face"
			נוקביה דאריך אנפין *Nukvei* *d'Arich Anpin*	[The female dimension of] "the Long Face"
chochmah	אבא *Abba*	"Father"	אבא עילאה *Abba Ila'ah*	"Supernal Father"
			אמא עילאה *Ima Ila'ah*	"Supernal Mother"
binah	אמא *Ima*	"Mother"	ישראל סבא *Yisrael Saba*	"Israel the Elder"
			תבונה *Tevunah*	"Understanding"
the midot	זעיר אנפין *Z'eir Anpin*	"The Small Face"	ישראל *Yisrael*	"Israel"
			לאה *Leah*	"Leah"
malchut	נוקביה דזעיר אנפין *Nukvei* *d'Z'eir Anpin*	"The Female of *Z'eir Anpin*"	יעקב *Yaakov*	"Jacob"
			רחל *Rachel*	"Rachel"

Both of the secondary, male and female *partzufim* of *Atik Yomin* and *Arich Anpin* exist within the same figure. There are thus actually only ten distinct secondary *partzufim*.

Within any particular *partzuf*, the *sefirot* are arranged along three axes, right, left and middle, as follows:

left axis	center axis	right axis
	keter	
binah		*chochmah*
	da'at	
gevurah		*chesed*
	tiferet	
hod		*netzach*
	yesod	
	malchut	

In this arrangement, there are three triads of related *sefirot*: *chochmah-binah-da'at* (the intellect), *chesed-gevurah-tiferet* (the primary emotions) and *netzach-hod-yesod* (the behavioral attributes).

Pesach (פסח, "Passover"): the seven-day *yom tov* (eight days in the Diaspora) commemorating the liberation of the Jewish people from Egyptian slavery.

Rachamim (רחמים, "mercy"): the inner experience of the *sefirah* of *tiferet*.

Rasha (רשע, "wicked one," pl. רשעים, *resha'im*): one who succumbs to his urge to do evil and commits a sin. He retains this status until he does *teshuvah, at which point he becomes a *ba'al teshuvah*.

Reisha d'Arich (רישא דאריך, "the head of *Arich [Anpin]*" [Aramaic]): the lowest of the three "heads" of *keter*, synonymous with the *partzuf* of *Arich Anpin*. In psychological terms, super-conscious will.

Reisha d'Ayin (רישא דאין, "the head of nothingness" [Aramaic]): the middle of the three "heads" of *keter*, related to the emotions of the *partzuf* of *Atik Yomin*. In psychological terms, super-conscious pleasure.

Reisha d'lo Ityada (רישא דלא אתידע [Aramaic]): the highest of the three "heads" of *keter*, related to the *keter* and intellect of the *partzuf* of *Atik Yomin*. In psychological terms, super-conscious belief in God.

Rebbe (רבי, "my teacher"): 1. a term used to describe or address a teacher of Torah. 2. leader of a branch of the Chassidic movement.

Reshimu (רשימו, "residue," "impression"): the residual impression of the infinite Divine light that God withdrew from the vacated space resulting from the *tzimtzum*.

Rosh Chodesh (ראש חדש, "new month"): the first day of a Jewish month, a day of celebration.

Rosh HaShanah (ראש השנה, "beginning of the year"): the Jewish New Year, commemorating the creation of man on the sixth day of creation, a day of universal judgment.

Ruach (רוח, "spirit"): a level of the *soul.

Sabbath: see Shabbat.

Sefirah (ספירה, pl. ספירות, *sefirot*): a channel of Divine energy or life force. It is via the *sefirot* that God interacts with creation; they may thus be considered His "attributes."

There are altogether eleven *sefirot* spoken of in Kabbalistic literature. Inasmuch as two of them (*keter* and *da'at*) are two dimensions of a single force, the tradition generally speaks of only ten *sefirot*. Each *sefirah* also possesses an inner experience, as discussed in *Chassidut*. The order of the *sefirot* is depicted in the chart on the following page.

Originally emanated as simple point-like forces, the *sefirot* at a certain stage develop into full spectrums of ten sub-*sefirot*. Subsequent to this, they metamorphose into *partzufim*.

Sefirot are composed of "lights" and "vessels." The light of
any *sefirah* is the Divine flow within it; the vessel is the identity
that flow takes in order to relate to or create some aspect of the
world in a specific way. Inasmuch as all reality is created by
means of the *sefirot*, they constitute the conceptual paradigm for
understanding all reality.

name			inner experience	
keter	כתר	"crown"	1. אמונה 2. תענוג 3. רצון	1. "faith" 2. "pleasure" 3. "will"
chochmah	חכמה	"wisdom," "insight"	בטול	"selflessness"
binah	בינה	"understanding"	שמחה	"joy"
da'at	דעת	"knowledge"	יחוד	"union"
chesed	חסד	"loving-kindness"	אהבה	"love"
gevurah	גבורה	"strength," "might"	יראה	"fear"
tiferet	תפארת	"beauty"	רחמים	"mercy"
netzach	נצח	"victory," "eternity"	בטחון	"confidence"
hod	הוד	"splendor," "thanksgiving"	תמימות	"sincerity," "earnestness"
yesod	יסוד	"foundation"	אמת	"truth"
malchut	מלכות	"kingdom"	שפלות	"lowliness"

Sefirat HaOmer (ספירת העמר, "counting the *Omer*"): an *omer* is a
dry measure mentioned in the Torah, and refers specifically to
the measure of barley offered in the *Temple on the second

day of *Pesach*. Beginning with this day, the Jew is commanded to count the next forty-nine days, after which, on the fiftieth day, falls the holiday of *Shavuot*.

Sefirot: plural of *sefirah*.

Shabbat (שבת, "Sabbath"): the day of rest beginning sunset on Friday and ending at nightfall on Saturday.

Shacharit (שחרית, "morning"): the morning prayer service.

Shavuot (שבועות, "weeks"): the *yom tov* celebrating the wheat harvest and commemorating the giving of the Torah at Mt. Sinai.

Shechinah (שכינה, "indwelling"): the immanent Divine Presence that inheres within the universe, corresponding to the *sefirah* of *malchut*, the "feminine" aspect of Divinity.

Shema (שמע, "hear"): a compilation of three Biblical passages (Deuteronomy 6:4-9, 11:13-21, Numbers 15:37-41) beginning with this word, or sometimes, the first verse alone. The first verse is the fundamental profession of monotheism, "Hear O Israel, GOD is our God, GOD is one." We are commanded to recite the *Shema* twice daily, and it has been incorporated into the morning and evening services as well as the prayer said upon retiring at night. When reciting the first sentence, we are intended to consider ourselves ready to give up our lives rather than deny the oneness of God.

Shemini Atzeret (שמיני עצרת, "the eighth-day gathering"): the *yom tov* immediately following *Sukot*, marking the end of the festivals of the high-holiday season.

Soul: the animating life or consciousness within man (or any other creature, see *Sha'ar HaYichud VehaEmunah*, ch. 1). The Jew possesses an additional "Divine soul" which is focused on God and His concerns in creation.

The essence of the soul possesses five manifestations ("names"), as follows:

name			experience
yechidah	יחידה	"unique one"	unity with God
chayah	חיה	"living being"	awareness of God continually creating the world
neshamah	נשמה	"breath"	vitality of intelligence
ruach	רוח	"spirit"	vitality of emotion
nefesh	נפש	"created soul"	physical vitality

Sukot (סוכות, "huts," "booths"): the **yom tov* celebrating the ingathering of the harvest and commemorating the clouds of glory that accompanied the Jewish people on their desert trek after the exodus from Egypt.

Taharah (טהרה, ritual "purity"): the spiritual state in which one purified himself from a specific degree of **tumah* (or from *tumah* altogether), and is thus allowed to enter areas or touch, be touched by, or consume things or food he otherwise may not. In general, the process of attaining *taharah* involves some type of reaffirmation of life, such as immersion in a **mikveh*. The spiritual correlate to *taharah* is optimistic elation or joy in the service of God. See *tumah*.

Talmud: (תלמוד, "learning"): the written version of the greater part of the oral *Torah, comprising mostly legal but also much homiletic and even some explicitly mystical material.

The Talmud comprises the *Mishnah* and the *Gemara*. The *Mishnah* is the basic compendium of the laws (each known as a *mishnah*) comprising the oral Torah, redacted by Rabbi Yehudah the Prince in the second century CE. The *Mishnah* was elaborated upon over the next few centuries in the academies of the Holy Land and Babylonia; this material is the *Gemara*.

There are thus two Talmuds: the one composed in the Holy Land, known as the *Talmud Yerushalmi* ("The Jerusalem

Talmud"), completed in the third century, and the one composed in Babylonia, known as the *Talmud Bavli* ("The Babylonian Talmud"), completed in the sixth century.

The *Mishnah*—and *ipso facto* the Talmud—is divided into tractates. References to the *Mishnah* are simply the name of the tractate followed by the number of the chapter and individual *mishnah*. The Jerusalem Talmud was first printed in Venice, 1523-24. Although subsequent editions have generally followed the same pagination as this edition, it is nonetheless cited by chapter and *halachah* (i.e., individual *mishnah*) number, as is the *Mishnah*. References to it are therefore prefaced by "Y.," to distinguish them from references to the *Mishnah* itself. The Babylonian Talmud was first printed in its entirety in Venice, 1520-23, and subsequent editions have followed the same pagination as this edition, as well. References to the tractates of the *Talmud Bavli* are simply by tractate name followed by page and column ("a" or "b").

Temimut (תמימות, "sincerity"): 1. earnestness and sincerity, either in one's conduct with his fellow man or in his connection to God. 2. The inner experience of *hod.

Temple (or "Holy Temple"; Hebrew: בית המקדש, "house of the sanctuary"): The central sanctuary in Jerusalem which serves as the physical abode of the indwelling of God's Presence on earth and as the venue for the sacrificial service. The Temple is the focal point of one's spiritual consciousness. The first Temple was built by King Solomon (833 BCE) and destroyed by the Babylonians (423 BCE); the second Temple was built by Zerubabel (synonymous, according to some opinions, with Nehemiah, 353 BCE), remodeled by Herod and destroyed by the Romans (68 CE); the third, eternal Temple will be built by *Mashiach.

Teshuvah (תשובה, "return"): the return of the individual (or community), after a period of estrangement, to a state of oneness with God and commitment to serve Him by observing His Torah. See *Ba'al Teshuvah.*

Tevunah (תבונה, "comprehension"): the lower of the two secondary *partzufim* which develop from the *partzuf* of *Ima*, the higher one being *Ima Ila'ah* (אמא עלאה).

Tiferet (תפארת, "beauty"): the sixth of the ten *sefirot.*

Tishah b'Av (תשעה באב, "the ninth of *Av*"): fast day commemorating the destruction of the two Temples, which occurred on this day.

Tikun (תקון, "rectification," pl. תקונים, *tikunim*): 1. a state of perfection and order. 2. "The world of *Tikun*" is the *world that first manifests this state, which is synonymous with the world of *Atzilut* (and *Berudim*, see Worlds). 3. the spiritual process of liberating the fragments of Divine light trapped within the material realm, unconscious of God's presence, thereby restoring the world to its initially intended state of perfection. This is accomplished through the performance of *mitzvot.* 4. a remedy prescribed against the effects of committing a specific sin.

Tohu (תהו, "chaos"): 1. the primordial, unrectified state of creation. 2. "The world of *Tohu*" is the *world which manifests this state, synonymous with the initial, premature form of the world of *Atzilut.* It itself develops in two stages: a stable form (*Akudim*) followed by an unstable form (*Nekudim*, see Worlds). The world of *Tohu* is characterized by "great lights" entering premature "vessels," resulting in the "breaking of the vessels" (שבירת הכלים). See *Tikun.*

Torah (תורה, "teaching"): God's will and wisdom as communicated to man. It pre-existed creation, and God used the Torah as His blueprint in creating the world.

God certainly communicated the teachings of the Torah in some form to Adam, who then transmitted them orally from generation to generation. The Patriarchs studied and observed all the laws of the Torah. However, God "officially" gave the Torah to mankind in the year 1313 BCE (and during the ensuing 40 years) at Mt. Sinai through Moses. The Ten Commandments were pronounced in the presence of the entire Jewish people.

God gave the Torah at Sinai in two parts: the written Torah and the oral Torah. The written Torah originally consisted of the Five Books of Moses (the "Pentateuch"), the other books being added later (see Bible). The oral Torah was communicated together with the Five Books of Moses as an explanation of the laws and lore included in it. This material was later written down by the sages of the oral Torah in the form of the *Talmud, the *Midrash, and the *Zohar. (All references to "the sages" in this book refer to the sages who transmitted the oral Torah as recorded in these works.)

Tumah (טומאה, ritual "impurity"): a spiritual state contracted by someone or something under various circumstances and to various degrees, in which he is prohibited from entering various holy areas or touching, being touched by, or consuming various holy objects or foods. In general, the sources of *tumah* are in some way associated with death (or a missed chance for potential life) and the purification process involves some type of reaffirmation of life. The spiritual correlate to *tumah* is depression or despair. See *taharah*.

Triangle: the sum of all integers from 1 to a specific number. For example, the triangle of five ($\Delta 5$) is $1 \perp 2 \perp 3 \perp 4 \perp 5 = 15$.

Tzadik (צדיק, "righteous" person; pl. צדיקים, *tzadikim*): someone who has fully overcome the evil inclination of his animal soul (and converted its potential into good). See *beinoni, rasha*.

Tzimtzum (צמצום, "contraction"): the contraction and "removal" of God's infinite light in order to allow for creation of independent realities. The primordial *tzimtzum* produced the "vacated space" (חלל) devoid of direct awareness of God's presence. See *Kav* and *Reshimu*.

Vessels: see *sefirah*.

World (Hebrew: עולם): a spiritual level of creation, representing a rung on the continuum of consciousness or awareness of God. In general, there are four worlds: **Atzilut*, **Beriah*, **Yetzirah*, and **Asiyah*. In particular, however, these four worlds originate from a fifth, higher world, **Adam Kadmon*. All ten **sefirot* and twelve **partzufim* are manifest in each world; however, since there is a one-to-one correspondence between the worlds and the *sefirot*, a particular *sefirah* dominates in each world.

The world of *Atzilut* is fundamentally different from the three subsequent worlds in that in it there is no awareness of self *per se*, while the three lower worlds are progressive stages in the development of self-awareness.

The worlds correspond to the Name *Havayah* and the **sefirot* as follows:

the Name *Havayah*	world	dominant *sefirah*	level of consciousness
קוצו של י	אדם קדמון *Adam Kadmon* "Primordial Man"	*keter*	Divine will to create and plan of creation
י	אצילות *Atzilut* "Emanation"	*chochmah*	solely of God; no self-awareness
ה	בריאה *Beriah* "Creation"	*binah*	potential existence; formless substance
ו	יצירה *Yetzirah* "Formation"	*midot*	general existence; archetypes, species
ה	עשיה *Asiyah* "Action"	*malchut*	particular existence; individual creatures

In particular, the world of *Atzilut* develops out of *Adam Kadmon* in three stages (the names of which are taken from Genesis 30:10):

world		developmental stage	description	
עקודים *Akudim*	"bound," "striped"	ten lights in one vessel	stable chaos	תהו *Tohu*
נקודים *Nekudim*	"dotted," "spotted"	ten lights in ten vessels	unstable chaos, collapse	
ברודים *Berudim*	"patterned," "speckled"	ten lights in ten inter-included vessels	stable, mature rectification	תקון *Tikun*

Whenever unqualified reference is made to the world of *Atzilut*, its final, mature stage is meant. It should be noted as well that our physical universe is *below* and "enclothes" the final two *sefirot* (**yesod* and **malchut*) of the spiritual world of *Asiyah* referred to above.

Yechidah (יחידה, "single one"): the highest of the five levels of the *soul.

Yesod (יסוד, "foundation"): the ninth of the ten **sefirot*.

Yetzirah (יצירה, "formation"): one of the four *worlds.

Yisrael Saba (ישראל סבא, "Israel the Elder" [Aramaic]): the lower of the two secondary **partzufim* which develop from the *partzuf* of **Abba*, the higher being *Abba Ila'ah* (אבא עלאה, "the higher *Abba*").

Yom Kippur (יום כפור, "Day of Atonement"): the holiest day of the Jewish year, marked by fasting and **teshuvah*, particularly through confession of sin.

Yom Tov (יום טוב, "good day" or "holiday"): a festive holiday on which, with certain exceptions, weekday work is prohibited just as on *Shabbat.

Z'eir Anpin (זעיר אנפין, "the small face" [Aramaic]): the **partzuf* of the **midot*, corresponding to the emotive faculties of the soul. In general, the concept of "finitude" or "finite power" is identified with *Z'eir Anpin*.

Zohar (זהר, "Brilliance"): The classic text of Kabbalah, by Rabbi Shimon bar Yochai (2nd century). The Zoharic literature includes the *Zohar* proper, the **Tikunei Zohar*, and the **Zohar Chadash*. The *Zohar* was printed in 1558 in both Mantua and Cremona, but standard pagination follows the Mantua edition.

Index